THE CIGAR ENTHUSIAST

The Definitive Guide to Selecting, Storing and Smoking Cigars

THE CIGAR ENTHUSIAST

The Definitive Guide to Selecting, Storing and Smoking Cigars

SONIA WEISS

BERKLEY BOOKS, NEW YORK

This book is an original publication of The Berkley Publishing Group.

THE CIGAR ENTHUSIAST

A Berkley Book / published by arrangement with
the author

PRINTING HISTORY
Berkley trade paperback edition/September 1997

The Putnam Berkley World Wide Web site address is
http://www.berkley.com

ISBN: 0-425-15981-7

BERKLEY®
Berkley Books are published by The Berkley Publishing Group,
200 Madison Avenue, New York, New York 10016,
a member of Penguin Putnam Inc.
BERKLEY and the "B" design
are trademarks belonging to Berkley Publishing Corporation.

PRINTED IN THE UNITED STATES OF AMERICA

10 9 8 7 6 5 4 3 2 1

CONTENTS

*To my father, with whom I will always
associate the aroma of a fine cigar.*

*And to Jim, my husband, who was
with me every step of the way.*

ACKNOWLEDGMENTS

All books come about through the contributions of many. This one is no different. Many, many thanks to:

Jessica Faust and the other fine folks at Berkley, who gave me the opportunity to indulge my passion for a good smoke and amplify it in print.

Sheree Bykofsky, agent extraordinaire, who believed it could happen when I was sure it wouldn't (more than once).

Matt Green and Mary Arlinghaus, a.k.a. WINE BOSS and MaryApp, the mavens of America Online's Cigar and Pipe message boards, and the countless other contributors to AOL's cigar boards, for their knowledge, insights, and willingness to share.

Natalie Voss, for lending her Internet-exploring skills and infinite patience to the section on on-line resources.

Mike Ford, a.k.a. Pinkster, who has smoked more cigars than anyone deserves to in one lifetime, and who was always willing to share his vast knowledge of them.

Rich Perelman, publisher of *Perelman's Pocket Cyclopedia of Cigars*, for sharing the manuscript on his cyclopedia of Cuban cigars before it went to press.

Jon Cacherat and the members of the Mystic Knights of the Leaf at Prince Phillips in Denver, who graciously welcomed me to their circle and into their humidor at the very beginning.

Steve and Stuart Bruckman at Havana's Fine Cigars in Denver, who also welcomed a woman into their midst and forgave the momentary mental lapses caused by my preoccupation with a certain writing project.

INTRODUCTION

The Making of a Cigar Enthusiast

Like many female cigar smokers, my passion for cigars and the rituals surrounding them was shaped by the men in my life—beginning with my father and my uncle, who both loved cigars and preferred them to all other forms of tobacco. Some of my fondest memories recall the two of them sitting at my grandmother's table in Miami Beach after a family meal, trimming and lighting their most recent acquisitions from some local shop. They were big men and they smoked big cigars, and I'd watch, transfixed, as they would talk and gesture, their cigars tipped with impossibly long ashes that seemed to defy gravity.

At home, I was often dispatched to fetch my father's 'gars, as he always called them, and I would linger over the task, inhaling the cedary smell of the cigar box as I plucked one out, rolling my selection between my fingers as I held it up to my nose, trying to smell it through its cellophane wrapper and imagining its aroma once it was unwrapped. As I reached my teens, my father showed me how to trim the head and, once, I actually lit one for him. Coughing and sputtering, those first few puffs were more than I could bear. Dad never told me I shouldn't inhale! Maybe that was his intent. I kept a respectful distance from then on, reserving my cigar experiences to fetching them for Dad and enjoying the aroma when others smoked.

In high school, I was one of the few people I knew who didn't smoke, but then came college and I joined the crowd, forming my nicotine habit over late-night term papers and computer terminals at the local newspaper where I worked as an intern. In public, I mostly smoked cigarettes, feeling they were more acceptable. At home I preferred cigarillos—the name of which now escapes me— that I would share with my decathalete boyfriend, who liked to smoke them after competition. On occasion, we'd supplement our cigarillos with Swisher Sweets: cheap, definitely sweet, and easily obtained at the local drug store.

As a young adult, I primarily stuck to cigarettes, reserving my enjoyment of cigars to a few puffs off my father's (by then, I figured out how to enjoy them without inhaling) or the occasional cigar shared with one of several male friends who smoked. I rarely smoked cigars in public—only when I was accompanying a gentleman to dinner—and I seldom bought them for myself. When I did, they were often last-minute purchases of whatever was available at the local drugstore.

In the fall of 1986, I had what was then and is still to this day my one and only asthma attack. Looking back, I know it was due to nerves and a great deal of stress, but at the time the only plausible medical explanation for this sudden attack was rampant, undiagnosed allergies, coupled with a bad case of bronchitis. And, of course, I was a smoker. My cigarette habit was up to about a pack a day— certainly not awful but significant all the same—and I had continued smoking cigars as well, usually in the company of the reporters with whom I worked at the time. "Your smoking days are over," the pulmonary specialist informed me once my breathing had returned to normal. I was too frightened to ask if that included cigars, and I'm sure he would have said yes if I had asked.

I quit smoking all forms of tobacco. The cigarettes I never missed because I never liked how they smelled or tasted anyway. And the way they stank up my clothes and hair—yuck! But cigars . . . well, that was another story. As time passed, I realized how much I missed their aroma. I missed watching their smoke lazily curl and swirl about. I missed the feel of them between my fingers. During this time, my father stopped smoking as well, and even my passive enjoyment of cigars seemed lost forever.

Nowhere did I read and at no time did anyone ever mention to me that there might be differences between cigarettes and cigars, and that smoking cigars might not pose as great a health risk as cigarettes. But as time passed, I began to question my absolute abstinence. Years had gone by without so much as a wheeze. I had weaned myself off all asthma medications and had adopted a much healthier and less stressful lifestyle. I toyed with the idea of *maybe* smoking a cigar. I was working as a reporter and freelance writer, and one of my indulgences at the end of a long day was kicking back in my big easy chair with a glass of bourbon, sipping it slowly and making it last through the long night ahead. Somehow, the hand not holding the glass seemed empty without a cigar. I'd imagine one of my father's big Churchills there, the blue smoke curling lazily about, complementing the mood as well as the bourbon. I wanted cigars to reoccupy a part of my life.

I was far from being alone. Cigars were making a comeback, and I began reading about smokers' nights being held at restaurants across the country: high-powered affairs with handsome men and—increasingly—elegant, exquisitely well-groomed women, always pictured with premium cigars between their manicured fingers. Certainly a far cry from the rural town where I was living and working.

One night, as my husband-to-be and I were returning from an evening out, we stopped to fill the car with gas. As he returned to the car, he tossed a pack of Swisher Sweets in my lap. "They seem to fit the mood," he said to my highly surprised expression. I quickly lit one up, threw back my head, and smiled as the familiar fragrance filled the air. Damn, it tasted good! I knew I had waited far too long.

This book is written for those of you who have waited too long as well. Whether you are male or female, a novice cigar smoker or wanting to return to cigars after quitting as I did, you owe it to yourself to experience the joys of cigar smoking.

There are hundreds of different brands of premium cigars on the market today—no one seems to know for sure the exact count, but it seems to be around 500 or so—offering smokers a wider choice in smoking experiences than ever before possible. And those experiences definitely aren't relegated to specific areas in men's clubs or the privacy of your own home. More and more restaurants and bars are recognizing the increasing numbers of people who wish to enjoy cigars in public and are offering specials smokers' nights and cigar dinners or rooms or special areas set aside especially for cigar smokers.

With the surge of interest in premium cigars have also come some setbacks. Today's overwhelming demand for handmade cigars has caused a tremendous backlog in filling orders. Many manufacturers truly cannot keep up with the demand or are unwilling to modify their production methods to do so. Prices are going up, selections are sometimes extremely limited, especially for the more popular brands, and more cigars are being rushed to market without the aging they once would have received to assure the best product quality.

However, none of this should deter you from entering the world of cigar smoking, because there's so much more there than just smoking cigars. Step into this world and you become a member of a fraternity, a brotherhood, a community of people who feel passionately about it. I have found my reentry into the world of cigar smoking an immensely enriching and enjoyable experience, filled with men and women united by their love of cigars and their desire to share that love with others. Some I've met at my local tobacconists. Others at restaurants and clubs. And still others, many others in fact, in cyberspace.

For all of the good things about cigar smoking, there are some facts that can't be denied. Although cigar smoking is becoming more popular by the day, the people who smoke them aren't necessarily enjoying the same popularity. Yes, private clubs and special smoking rooms at public clubs and restaurants are also becoming more popular, but there's still a great deal of prejudice against cigar smokers in other public places that do allow other forms of smoking.

And there's the medical debate. Although most medical studies have concluded that cigar smoking doesn't pose as great a risk as smoking cigarettes does, there are still risks involved any time you indulge in any kind of tobacco product. Because premium cigars contain naturally cured tobacco, and because they aren't doctored up with chemical or nicotine additives, many people will argue that a light cigar habit—meaning one a day or so—probably doesn't present a significant health concern for an otherwise healthy individual. I fall into the light cigar habit category, and, I guess, I'm willing to take my chances.

It appears as though more and more people are willing to do so these days. Dealing with the stresses caused by our fast-paced society almost forces us to search for ways to take time out. The time spent enjoying a good cigar can almost be meditative, and I'm in agreement with female cigar smoker and novelist George Sand, who wrote, "The cigar numbs the sorrow and fills the solitary hours with a million gracious images." For me, giving a cigar its proper due requires a focus that eliminates and silences the world beyond the cigar. I relish my cigar smoking time.

Writing this book was a journey of sorts for me. Although my purpose in writing it was to share what knowledge I have of cigars and my love of a good smoke with beginning cigar enthusiasts, it became more. I began it as an occasional smoker—maybe two or three cigars a week—with somewhat limited knowledge, primarily based on my relationships with several tobacconists where I live. As I began writing and researching, I tapped into a wealth of resources I never knew existed, and I very definitely expanded my window of experience. (I guess it goes without saying that my smoking habits changed somewhat as well—it's tough to spend all your time thinking and writing about cigars without wanting to smoke them more often.) There's an immense collective memory when it comes to cigar smoking, and the amount of information about all aspects of cigars is deep and vast. Small wonder, when you consider the cigar's long history in this country, as well as its role as a cultural icon.

Although I began my second affiliation with cigars by smoking a machine-made cigar—a Swisher Sweet—I very quickly moved to premium handmade brands because they were a greater reminder of the cigars of my childhood memories. Today, my love of cigars is very much shaped by the wide variety of premium handmade brands that are on the market. This is the fastest-growing segment of the cigar industry today, and the bulk of this book focuses on the enjoyment of them. This isn't to say there aren't good machine-made cigars that you should consider trying, because there are, and some of the venerable old machine-made brands are still the preferred cigars for many smokers. George Burns, for example, who could afford to smoke any cigar he chose, will always be remembered for smoking El Productos, machine-made in Puerto Rico, which he liked because they were mild and they stayed lit while he was on stage. You'll find varying selections of machine-made cigars at most tobacconists because they often present a good value for the price, and you'll soon learn the difference between these cigars and what you might encounter at the corner drug store.

I don't profess to be an expert on cigars. Many people are, and you'll find information about them and what they have to offer in the resources section of this book. What I do feel I am is an informed guide, as well as a dedicated cigar enthusiast, and it is in this context that I offer my services to lead you in your own cigar discovery journey as, hopefully, you will also become a cigar enthusiast. And like all good journeys, it must begin at the beginning . . .

CIGARS AND YOUR HEALTH

Is cigar smoking as dangerous as using other forms of tobacco? Opinions on this vary, but the general consensus seems to be that, while using tobacco in any form has its risks, smoking a cigar or two a day, and not inhaling them, doesn't pose a significant health risk for people in good health.

Tobacco was first suspected as a carcinogen in the early 1900s when physicians began recording increases in the incidence of lung cancer cases. Since that time, tobacco's effects on the heart and lungs has been the focus of innumerable studies, spawning a number of published reports and articles. Because of the popularity of cigarettes, many of these articles focus on cigarette use and cancer; cigar smoking is rarely specifically addressed, and those articles that do address it make little, if any, distinction between the risks of smoking machine-made versus handmade cigars.

Will smoking a cigar hurt my computer?

I have yet to hear of a computer contracting cancer from a cigar. You'd have to smoke a lot of cigars, and probably in a very small room, for the oils in cigar smoke to damage a computer. If you do, and you're in a small room, you may want to use a small fan or air purifier.

Of these reports, the one that caused the greatest impact on smoking habits in the United States was the Surgeon General's landmark report on smoking and health released in January 1964, which dealt a strong blow to cigarette smoking. After the release of this report, millions of Americans switched to cigars or pipes. I'll never forget the sight of my mother smoking a corncob pipe! Cigar consumption, by the way, peaked at an all-time high of 9.1 billion that year. Numbers declined steadily after 1964, as many cigarette smokers returned to their original habit, or, perhaps, quit smoking altogether. Those who did substitute cigars or pipes for their favorite cigarettes often found it difficult to not inhale these substitutions due to years of deeply inhaling their cigarettes. It can be assumed that, for these people, the risk of lung cancer and other diseases most likely did not diminish.

Marc J. Schneiderman, M.D., a cigar smoker himself, has researched the findings in numerous articles on tobacco and smoking research studies. In an excellent paper based on eighteen of the articles that he felt contained the most relevant information on cigar smoking, he concludes that moderate, noninhaled cigar use poses no significant health threat.

Obviously, the key words here are *moderate* and *noninhaled*.

Certainly, what constitutes a moderate habit to one person may be a significant habit to another. Cigar size is also a factor to consider when discussing moderation. Although inhaling cigars is never recommended, I think it's somewhat common to take in a little smoke on occasion; certainly, milder cigars can easily be inhaled without the coughing and sputtering associated with fuller-bodied smokes.

I quit smoking cigarettes a long time ago, but now would like to try a cigar. Will it reawaken my interest in cigarettes?

This was a question I asked of other cigar smokers and ex-cigarette smokers. For most, the differences between cigars and cigarettes are significant enough to not reawaken the desire for cigarettes. A few admitted to still indulging in an occasional cigarette as well, but at nowhere near the level they were at when they were confirmed cigarette smokers, and not as a result of their cigar smoking. As for myself, I have found the return to cigars very enjoyable, and I have not desired cigarettes one bit. I can also go for quite some time without smoking a cigar and not crave them.

As an ex-cigarette smoker, I approached my return to cigars with some hesitation, not knowing if enjoying an occasional cigar would awaken any long-dormant urges for cigarettes. Happily to say, this hasn't happened, and in discussing the issue with other former cigarette smokers, the same seems to hold true for them as well. However, the consensus also seems to be that you should stay away from all forms of tobacco if you're trying to quit smoking cigarettes.

If you want to find out more about the relationship of cigars to cancer and other health issues, Schneiderman's findings and synopses of the eighteen articles can be found on the World Wide Web (check chapter 8 for the exact address). He also provides a lengthy reference list of articles for anyone wanting to delve further into this topic.

I'm trying to quit smoking. Would having a cigar instead of a cigarette help?

I asked this question of several other cigar smokers, many of them ex-cigarette smokers. The overwhelming consensus was *no!* If you're trying to quit smoking, quit trying, and quit! Stay away from tobacco in all forms until you know for sure that you've broken the nicotine addiction.

1

The History of a "Bewitching Vegetable"

A small cigar can change the world I know . . .

IAN ANDERSON (JETHRO TULL)

The recorded history of cigars very conveniently begins with something we all know at least a little something about, and that's the discovery of the New World by Christopher Columbus. When Columbus and his sailors landed in the West Indies, they were greeted by natives carrying wooden spears and bearing gifts of fruit and—you guessed it—tobacco for the newcomers. Having never seen (or smelled) anything like it, Columbus and his men made quick business of the unknown, funny looking brown stuff. They kept the fruit.

It took Columbus and his group several more encounters with the residents of the New World to understand that the dried out, odd-smelling vegetal substance was a prized commodity among the inhabitants of this new continent. During their explorations, they observed several forms of tobacco use: after a trek across Cuba while searching for the Grand Khan, two of his sailors, Luis de Torres and Rodrigo de Jeres (some historical references also spell his last name Xeres), reported seeing a group of Indians smoking what now fits the description of a crude cigar, albeit quite a large one, wrapped in a large leaf of palm or maize.

Tobacco consumption was nothing new to the inhabitants of North America and the islands that constituted Columbus's New World. Stone carvings, dating back many centuries, document the use of tobacco in various forms in religious and social ceremonies in Central America and Mexico. The dried leaf was called by various names depending on the region and the tribe, but everyone had a word for it and a variety of different ways of using it. Crude cigars were popular, but chewing, inhaling, and smoking it through various types of pipes made of clay or gourds also was common.

Several strains of tobacco grew profusely in many areas of the New World. *Nicotiana rustica,* or yellow henbane, a small-leaved, bitter tobacco, was cultivated by many tribes in North America. *Nicotiana tabacum,* a tall, broad-leaved, milder strain, grew in the more temperate climes of Central and South America. It would evolve into the tobacco we know today.

Tobacco use was so prevalent in the New World that it didn't escape the notice of any of the early explorers, each of whom documented what they saw in somewhat wondrous and incredulous terms. The popularity of this strange commodity was clear; what they didn't understand was why it was being used. Was it for ritual or medicinal purposes? Pleasure and enjoyment? Some interesting misconceptions and prejudices about tobacco's use sprang from these accounts, which would greatly govern tobacco's acceptance when it crossed the Atlantic Ocean and was introduced to the inhabitants of the Old World.

BACK TO THE OLD WORLD

Various Spanish and Portuguese explorers took tobacco back to their countries of origin, although it's not quite certain who was the first to do so. Rodrigo de Jeres, however, is celebrated by his hometown of Ayamonte as the first person to smoke in Europe. (He was also probably the first to be imprisoned for his public smoking habits, after the henchmen of the Inquisition saw him enjoying his habit a bit too much. It was said that he was harboring a devil.)

Once across the Atlantic, tobacco met with mixed success and acceptance. Residents of the Old World didn't quite know what to make of this discovery, and they certainly didn't understand why it was such an important economic and social commodity in the New World. After all, it wasn't gold or a precious spice, the value of both long acknowledged and established in their world. To many, tobacco was to be feared, as it was associated with heathen rituals from a part of the world they knew little about.

Tobacco did gain acceptability, however, as a therapeutic herb, and a litany of ailments was developed that cigar smoking would ostensibly cure, including asthma, headaches, bites, colds, and rheumatism. One of the first to proclaim the virtues of tobacco as a poultice was a relative of a page employed by Jean Nicot, the French ambassador at the Portuguese court. Nicot, who would later classify the plant and earn the right to name it, sent seeds of the plant to Catherine de'Medici, the Queen Mother of France. The leaves grown from these seeds reportedly cured ailing Frenchmen, and the therapy came to be known as Nicotiane.

During this time, tobacco was introduced to other European countries as well; Holland, at the time a Spanish possession, eagerly embraced what was called the "bewitching vegetable." Dutch seamen also smuggled tobacco to England, sparking that country's interest in what was coming to be called "Spanish gold" for its ever-increasing trade value in other parts of the world and spurring its cultivation as a crop in the British colonies that would soon be established in America.

Although tobacco was best accepted for its therapeutic qualities by most Europeans, its social pleasures were beginning to be understood as well. Mostly, it was chewed or smoked in pipes as the skills necessary to wrap cigars were virtually nonexistent outside of the Spanish West Indies or Cuba. In Spain and Portugal however, cigars were plentiful, due to the tobacco-producing colonies these countries had established in the West Indies and Brazil, where cigars and palm-wrapped cigarettes were the preferred modes of tobacco consumption. Soon, their popularity would spread to Europe as well, when French and British soldiers, fighting in Spain during the

Napoleonic Wars, became acquainted with cigar smoking and carried numerous cigars away with them once the fighting was over; the high taxes Britain imposed on these cigars, however, reserved them as a luxury for the aristocracy who could afford them. The duty was reduced in 1829, and many Old English snuffboxes were put aside in favor of this novel new smoking form.

The vogue for cigars steadily increased, spawning the establishment of a smoking room in the House of Commons, the precursor to the soon-to-be-popular smoking rooms in London clubs and smoking cars on British trains, established to help Victorian men keep their smoking habits away from the dainty ladies of the time. By the end of the nineteenth century, the after-dinner cigar, with port or brandy, had become a firmly established British tradition.

What is a divan?

Dating back to Victorian London, divans are rooms specifically set aside for smoking, often cigars. Back in Victorian days, they featured comfortable chairs and sofas, hence the name. Befitting the style of the time, Victorian divans were decidedly Oriental in style.

The cigarette, introduced to England and France in the 1850s, almost put the death to cigars on the Continent. Essentially a paper-wrapped cigar, they had been developed in Spain, where various wrappers had been experimented with to make small cigars. Although their success helped bolster smoking in all forms, it was also easier to roll your own cigarettes than buy ready-made cigars, and resources began to be devoted to manufacturing cigarettes. By the start of World War I, almost half the tobacco imported to Britain was made into cigarettes.

WHILE BACK IN AMERICA . . .

The first tobacco plantations in the New World were established in Virginia by colonist John Rolfe, who, after trying unsuccessfully to cultivate the small-leaved and bitter *Nicotiana rustica,* switched to *Nicotiana tabacum* in 1612. It is not known how Rolfe received the seed of the large-leaved Spanish plant, but his switch to it would prove to be a propitious choice as, just two years later, Virginia was supplying one pound of tobacco to London for every twenty supplied by the Spanish.

Pipes were the preferred way of using tobacco in the American colonies. The cigar wouldn't make its appearance for over another 100 years, when Israel Putnam, at the time an officer in the British army, returned from King George III's war in Cuba with three donkey loads of Havana cigars. (Putnam, by the way, would go on to become an American general in the Revolutionary War).

Putnam's home was in Connecticut, where early settlers had begun growing tobacco in the seventeenth century after observing its cultivation by the Indian tribes of the region. Soon, a homemade-cigar trade was established, with farmers and their families rolling their own cigars with rough homegrown leaf. These cigars, crude and unbanded, were used in trade for store goods and became an integral part of the economy. They would eventually be packed in barrels, either by the farmers who made them or the storekeepers who took them in trade, and shipped to East Coast ports, where they met a ready market with sailors and other port workers. Before long, small cigar factories were established in Connecticut; the crude quality of the cigars produced in these factories took a significant turn for the better when, in 1810, an enterprising local cigar manufacturer in Suffield imported a Cuban cigar-roller to teach the fine points of cigar construction to American hands.

By the Revolutionary War, cigar manufacturing had spread from rural locations to such cities as New York and Philadelphia. In Conestoga, Pennsylvania, long, slender cigars were being made from local tobacco, called shoestring. They resembled the spokes on the wheels of the covered wagons that were also being manufactured there, and came to be called stogies for their resemblance. Pencil-thin long-nines and short-sixes, and supers, similar to modern cigars but finished with a twist, were other styles fashioned from the rough leaf grown in this region and were often distributed free to steady customers in taverns and pubs. Although a few cigars carried brand names, most did not.

Cuban cigars and tobacco, still far superior to any variety grown in America, were also being exported to America during this period. The tobacco was used to fashion what were called half-Spanish cigars, which were probably the first cigars to bear a resemblance to today's handmade cigars as they combined a Connecticut wrapper with a binder and filler blended from other leaves, including some Cuban. As early as 1810, the cigar makers of Philadelphia, rolling about thirty million cigars per year, were using what they called Spanish tobacco in one out of every ten cigars, probably putting West Indian wrappers on cigars made with Kentucky filler. Clear Havanas, made completely with Cuban leaf, were too expensive for the mass market, although they started to be manufactured in the 1840s. They would sell at four to five times the price of domestic cigars.

The growing sophistication of American smokers would spur increased importation of Cuban leaf, usually through New York, where sugar importers had at one time treated it as an inconsequential sideline to their main business. By the 1850s, some two to five and a half million pounds per year were entering the country. During this period, American growers began experimenting with the qualities of the tobacco being grown in Connecticut, eventually producing a plant with smoother, more attractive leaves that made better wrappers than the shoestring tobacco previously used. This Connecticut broadleaf, as it was soon called, created a wrapper style that is still in great demand today. Improved curing processes, largely derived from Cuban processes, were also applied to this new tobacco. Production of it grew from 540,000 pounds in 1830 to 9,300,000 pounds in 1859.

The U.S. cigar industry continued to expand, largely aided by the numbers of proficient cigar makers among the growing tides of Europeans immigrating to the United States who had manufactured cigars in their native countries. New markets for those cigars swelled when soldiers returned from the Mexican War of 1846–47 with a newfound admiration for cigars. The annexation of California in 1848 brought even more enthusiasts to the world of cigar smoking, as gold prospectors, eager to celebrate their discoveries, adopted the ancient Mexican-Spanish customs practiced by the native Californios and lit up fine cigars.

By this time, cigar production had become a full-fledged industry in Cuba, where there were 9,500 tobacco plantations and a number of cigar factories in Havana and other cities. Products from these factories as well as loose tobacco were exported mainly to the United States until tariff barriers were established in 1857. During the same period, brand and size differentiation began, and the cigar box and band were introduced.

Who invented the cigar band?

Various people are credited with this one. Most give the credit to a Dutchman, Gustave Bock, one of the first Europeans to get involved in the Havana cigar industry, somewhat after the introduction of the cigar box and labels, and for the same reason: to distinguish his brand from the many others on the market.

By the 1880s, there wasn't a state or territory in the U.S. (except for Montana and Idaho) that didn't manufacture cigars, although the major production of them was centered in ten major cigar manufacturing areas, including Philadelphia, New York, Baltimore, Cincinnati, Hartford County in Connecticut, St. Louis, Hampden County in Massachusetts, Newark, Albany, and New Orleans. By 1880, there were 53,000 cigar makers in the United States; New York City alone had 14,500 people working in cigar factories. Interestingly, the southern United States was home to very little cigar manufacturing activity until after the Civil War, instead focusing its tobacco production on plug and twist. This would change when, during the 1890s, many Cuban cigar makers, faced with the growing political upheaval caused by Cuba's struggle for independence from Spain, emigrated to Jamaica and Florida. Cuban immigrants began a flourishing manufacturing center in Tampa during the 1890s, where millions of half-Havanas and clear-Havanas were produced at half the cost of Cuban-made imports for the eager American market.

What's the purpose of a cigar band?

Its main purpose is to distinguish one brand of cigar from another. In Victorian times, it was thought that the bands protected smokers' fingers from becoming stained (important when gentlemen wore white evening gloves). Some claim the band helps hold the cigar together, although no properly constructed cigar should need such help. Bands at the foot of the cigar are thought to help protect the delicate foot of the cigar.

THE 1900s

By the turn of the century, tobacco use of all kinds in the United States was increasing; per person cigar consumption reached its all-time peak in 1907. After that year, cigarette smoking would begin to supplant the cheaper cigar brands, bringing a less-expensive, more convenient way of enjoying smoking to the masses. Cigars started to become luxury items reserved for after-dinner enjoyment; they became somewhat out of place in the accelerating pace that was beginning to characterize America's bigger cities. Regional manufacturing all but disappeared as America's tobacco resources were increasingly being earmarked for the large southern cigarette manufacturers. The First World War would deliver another staggering blow to America's cigar manufacturing, as this most compact and convenient smoking form hit the trenches with American doughboys, building a generation of dedicated cigarette smokers.

"A GOOD FIVE-CENT CIGAR"

Woodrow Wilson's Vice President Thomas Riley Marshall was indeed the one who uttered these famous words, as an aside to a Senate secretary following a long oration about the needs of the country by a senator from Kansas. And, at that time, five cents could buy you a good cigar. However, they couldn't compete with cigarettes that sold for less than a cent a piece. The growing popularity of cigarettes continued to threaten America's cigar manufacturers. Determined to recover or at least keep its market share, cigar manufacturers looked at ways they could compete. The obvious solution was to develop cigar-making machinery so that cheap, mass-produced cigars could compete with cheap, mass-produced cigarettes. By 1929, about a third to a half of the cigars produced in the United States were machine-made, many of them with Havana leaf. Selling for about five cents for three cigars, they were now an affordable smoke for laborers and everyday workingmen.

Mechanization may have helped stave off the cigar's fall from favor, but it dealt a death blow to America's handmade cigar industry. Small cigar shops began to disappear as cigar machine manufacturers extolled the virtues of mechanized production. By 1958, there were fewer than 600 cigar factories in the United States. This number would continue to dwindle in the years to come.

CASTRO AND THE DIASPORA OF THE CUBAN CIGAR INDUSTRY

In 1959, Fidel Castro lead a successful revolution against General Fulgencio Batista. Following the revolution, he nationalized Cuban and foreign assets, including the country's cigar industry.

Although the United States had supported Castro's efforts in deposing Batista, his actions after the revolution lead President John F. Kennedy to impose a trade embargo in 1962. This meant that neither Cuban tobacco nor Havana cigars could be legally imported into the United States, except in small quantities for personal use by certain individuals. (Prior to imposing the embargo, however, Kennedy assured his personal supply of Cuban cigars by dispatching Pierre Salinger, his press secretary, on a mission to secure as many Cuban cigars as he could from area merchants.)

Many dispossessed factory owners fled Cuba in hopes of starting up production again in more favorable areas. As a result, cigars bearing Cuban brand names are today made in the Dominican Republic, Miami, Honduras, and Mexico. Aside from their similarities in name, there's little relationship between these cigars and their Havana counterparts.

As Cuban cigars faded away from the American consciousness, sales of other cigars continued to decline as well. Aside from a rally in 1964 following the release of the Surgeon General's report on the hazards of cigarette smoking, when cigar sales in the United States hit an all-time high of 9 billion, they steadily decreased to just 2.3 billion in 1992. Decreases in the sales of mass market, machine-produced cigars accounted for most of the decline.

There was still a number of premium cigar smokers in the United States, but many of them kept their cigar-smoking habits fairly quiet as antismoking activity swept across the nation in the '60s, '70s, and '80s, largely spurred by the release of more reports detailing the findings from continuing research on the relationship of tobacco to cancer. It took a great deal of intestinal fortitude to ward off the attacks that were often launched, both verbally and nonverbally, at any smoker indulging his or her habit in public, regardless of smoking preference. It just was easier to light up at home, and this is where many smokers began to rediscover the peace and relaxation that a good cigar can deliver.

THE SCENE TODAY

Although cigar sales continued to drop through the early 1990s, the number of premium cigar smokers in America had slowly but steadily increased since the mid-1970s (they were just smoking less cigars than their earlier counterparts). A renaissance of sorts was quietly taking place fueled by these smokers; in 1992, they gained a voice with the debut of an unusual upscale magazine. Called *Cigar Aficionado*, it celebrated premium cigars, the lifestyles of those who enjoyed them, and many other fine things in life. And it hit a chord. Long-time cigar smokers no longer felt it necessary to disguise or hide their enjoyment of cigars. Celebrities began appearing in public with their favorite cigars. Curiosity about cigar smoking increased among those who didn't smoke or who had quit smoking cigarettes, fueling an increase in cigar sales during the latter months of 1992 that continues to grow today. Suddenly, cigar smoking, for many years the subject of disgrace and scorn, didn't seem like the world's worst thing to do, and many people were intrigued by what cigars might have to offer.

Today, sales of premium cigars continue to skyrocket as tobacco growers and manufacturers struggle to keep up with the unprecedented demand for their products. The ranks of smokers of premium cigars continue to grow as well, as more and more people find that the enjoyment of a good cigar can add a special dimension to their lives. Although you may hear some old-time smokers grumble about the stresses placed on cigar supplies by these new smokers, they're very much the driving force behind the continuing evolution of the cigar industry as it looks ahead to the markets of the future.

My girlfriend and I enjoy sharing a cigar, but I don't enjoy sharing her lipstick. Would it be bad form for me to suggest she remove her lipstick before we light up?

Absolutely not! But she may not like the idea if she's in full makeup and out in public with you. Another way to get around lipstick rings on a cigar is to suggest that she purse her lips slightly and insert the cigar just past her lips when it's her turn to take a puff. This should hold the lipsticked part of her lips away from the cigar.

WHAT LIES AHEAD

Like all trends, cigar smoking has its faddish aspects, but these are bound to diminish over time as the people who embraced cigar smoking as the chic thing to do become tired of the fad and move on to something else. They'll leave behind a dedicated population of smokers—true cigar enthusiasts—that will continue to support today's cigar industry while enjoying the pure pleasure that only a premium cigar can offer. Hopefully, you'll be one of them.

2

The Making
of a Cigar

*Just as there are no two great wines which are the same,
no two cigars are identical.*

Zino Davidoff, *The Connoisseur's Book of the Cigar*

The cigar you hold in your hand today originated from a seed not much larger than the period at the end of this sentence. It most likely has taken at least several years to reach you, going through dozens of different stages and processes—and, yes, lots of hands—during its journey. Unless it's constructed entirely with tobaccos from one country—which would then designate it as a *puro*—chances are it represents a virtual geographical melting pot as well, with a wrapper from one country, the binder from another, and the filler comprised of tobaccos from several more.

WHERE TOBACCO GROWS

Various strains of tobacco grow all over the world. The plant is noted for its adaptability to a wide range of conditions and climates, which explains why you can find old cigar presses in antique stores as far north as Minnesota.

Aside from the various types of wrapper grown in Connecticut, most of the tobacco used in the production of cigars today originates from climates significantly more moderate than that of the northern United States. The same characteristics that make tobacco adaptable to various different climates and conditions also make it a very mutable and suggestible plant, which means that the characteristics of the soil where it is grown will distinguish its taste. Cigars with a preponderance of Dominican tobacco, for example, will taste significantly different from those with tobacco primarily grown in Honduras. The fertile soil of the Vuelta Abajo region in Cuba is said to have certain qualities that yield some of the best cigar tobacco in the world. Because of this, it's impossible to replicate the taste of a Cuban cigar with tobacco grown anywhere else, even if it's tobacco grown with seed that originally came from Cuba. It can come close, but it will still be an imitation of the real thing.

It's estimated that a single ounce of tobacco seeds contains some 300,000 seeds. Because they're so small, it's difficult to sow them directly into a field as you would other crops such as beans or corn. What happens instead is that they are planted first in special cold frames or hotbeds, where the tender seedlings can be cared for and watched over until they reach a size sufficient for transplanting. From their very beginning and throughout their development, tobacco plants lead a strict, regimented, even cosseted lifestyle. Their growth is constantly monitored, and the leaves that they will yield are inspected, sorted, and graded at every turn, assuring the greatest success in the curing and aging processes to come, and, hopefully, resulting in the highest-quality, most consistent tobacco product possible.

After about forty-five days of growing in their special beds, the small seedlings are transplanted to specially prepared fields and planted according to very exacting specifications to assure a standard size and quality for both the plants and their leaves. If the young plants are to yield shade-grown tobacco, they'll continue their life cycle under a canopy of cheesecloth or fine mesh, which serves as a sunscreen for the delicate seedlings, while providing them some protection from extremes in temperature as well.

Once they're transplanted, tobacco plants grow rapidly, especially if they have favorable growing conditions with the right mixture of sun and moisture. At maturity, they can measure as tall as six feet or more. The number and size of the leaves on each plant vary, but a single leaf can measure 24 by 18 inches. The leaves nearest the ground, called volado, are exposed to the least amount of light and tend to be mildest. Seco, from the middle of the plant, is medium in flavor and texture. Ligero, growing at the very top of the plant, reaps the most benefit from its growing conditions and is strongest in texture and taste. Since they all have different flavor levels and textures, leaves from all three parts of the tobacco plant are customarily blended when making cigars.

As they near maturity, tobacco plants begin to set flower heads, which are removed by the tobacco grower in order to put more energy into the development of the plant's leaves. At this point, the plants are almost ready for their first harvesting, which will remove anywhere from two to four leaves, usually beginning at the bottom of the plant as these leaves mature the fastest. Each plant may undergo as many as five to six harvestings, also referred to as primings, during its growing season; all told, each plant will yield between eight to twelve leaves, sometimes more, that may eventually end up as part of a cigar.

After the leaves are harvested, they are sorted by size and texture, braided together, and taken to curing barns, where, draped over long poles away from the sun, they will begin their first curing, aided by the gentle breezes of their native country. Lasting anywhere from three to eight weeks, this gradual process removes much of their moisture, and as they dry, the leaves change from their original green hue to yellow and eventually brown.

After they've completed their time in the curing barns, the leaves are shipped to packing houses, where they are again separated and graded by size, texture, and color. They'll then be tied into bundles of twenty, called hands, and prepared for their next stage of aging, fermentation.

MAKING THEM SWEAT

If left at the state they achieved during their time in the curing barns, tobacco leaves would resemble nothing more than the dried up, shriveled leaves that they are. Not much to look at, and definitely not something you'd like to smoke. Something has to happen to change the character of these leaves. And that something is fermentation—the breakdown of complex molecules in organic compounds, caused by the influence of a ferment—in this case, heat and water. If this sounds something like what happens in compost piles, you're right, but the process is stopped long before the tobacco reaches anything even remotely resembling what you might find in your backyard heap.

It is at this stage that the characteristics of the tobacco you will eventually smoke begin to emerge. The hands of tobacco are layered into tall piles, which are also called burros or bulks. The weight of the layers causes air to become trapped inside the bulk, and it begins to heat up. As the bulk gradually warms, the fermentation process gets under way as moisture, sap, and ammonia nitrate are released from the tobacco leaves. The leaves literally sweat—indeed, sweating is another name for this process—while undergoing immense physical changes as the starches in their leaves convert into plant sugars and they darken in color. Some leaves will produce more sugar than others, which is why some cigars will taste a little sweet when you light them.

Long thermometers, inserted into the bulk at routine intervals, are used to measure the progress of the fermentation process. Different tobaccos are allowed to reach different temperatures; for example, tobacco destined to become maduro wrappers is aged the longest and allowed to reach the highest temperature in order to reach its rich, dark color.

As the bulk cures and reaches its desired heat, the bottom leaves are moved to the top and the top leaves are moved to the bottom. This process, called turning or rotating, insures even fermentation throughout the bulk. Eventually, all the leaves in the bulk will have their turn on the top, middle, or bottom during the several months or so that it will take to achieve their final texture and color. When this occurs, each leaf is removed from the bulk, where it undergoes yet another inspection. At this point, the leaves are also graded according to the color they achieved during fermentation.

After fermentation, the tobacco is almost ready to be fashioned into cigars, but not quite. First, they must undergo yet another aging cycle, usually in cigar factory warehouses, where the leaves, now formed into bales, will sit for several years or so, and sometimes longer. Some fermentation will continue at this point, but, most importantly, the leaves will continue to develop character.

At this point, the cured leaves are still fairly stiff and brittle. Moisture must be added back to them before they can withstand the rigors of being shaped into cigars. This is done by spraying the leaves with a fine mist of water once the bales are removed from storage. If the leaves have been cured with their stems intact, they are removed at this point.

One more inspection, a final sorting, and the leaves are ready to be fashioned into cigars.

CIGAR ANATOMY

Cigars are composed of three basic parts. Although the tobacco used in each part will vary, and it is the unique combination of these tobaccos that gives each cigar its character, all three parts are equally important in creating the unique characteristics that differentiate one cigar from the other.

Starting from the outside, we have:

The Wrapper
This is exactly what its name implies. It is the outside covering of the cigar, and, obviously, the first component we see when choosing or judging a cigar. Wrappers are fashioned from the finest leaves and vary considerably in their color, texture, feel, and aroma. The wrapper makes a significant contribution to the overall taste of a cigar.

The Binder

Lurking just beneath the wrapper, the binder is what holds the cigar together. It is usually made of a heavier leaf than the wrapper, and it is chosen to complement the wrapper and filler.

The Filler

This is the guts of the cigar. In premium cigars, you'll find what is called long filler, meaning that the tobacco leaves are left long and will run the entire length of the cigar. Less expensive cigars most often are made with short filler, bits and pieces of tobacco leaves that are chopped up and fashioned into filler. In larger ring gauge cigars, the filler can contain as many as five different types of tobacco.

ROLLING THEM UP

Premium handmade cigars are exactly what the name implies: They are shaped and rolled by hand. The cigar maker takes the filler blend—usually a carefully guarded secret—and forms what is called a bunch. It looks somewhat like the folds you might see in a curtain or like pleats in an accordian bellows. When done correctly, this process creates even channels of air that run the entire length of the cigar. It's a vital step in the construction of a cigar; if a bunch is gathered together too loosely, it will make a cigar that draws easily but burns fast, creating a hot, harsh smoke. If gathered tightly, it will be difficult to draw on, which cigar smokers refer to as a plugged cigar.

The cigar maker then places the filler on a binder leaf and rolls the two together. At this point, the combined leaves are beginning to resemble a cigar, albeit it one without a wrapper. Most cigars are then shaped in wooden molds, and then placed into presses that will further squeeze them into shape. Once molded into form, the cigars are removed from the mold and rolled into a wrapper leaf. Finally, a round piece of tobacco is used to fashion the cap, which is glued into place with goma, a flavorless gum derived from the tragacanth tree, and the cigar is cut to its final length.

Why are some cigars more difficult (or easier) to draw on than others?

An enjoyable cigar should provide you an easy smoke, but not too easy a smoke. In other words, the cigar should be easy to draw. But some can be incredibly hard, while others are so easy they burn and smoke too quickly.

Why this happens is often related to the way the cigar is put together. A tightly rolled cigar can be very difficult to draw, which can frustrate the smoker enough to want to put the cigar down right away. A loosely bunched cigar can draw more easily, but can also smoke very quickly and unevenly.

The age of the cigar and how it's been stored can also affect its smoking ease. Younger cigars can often be more difficult to draw. A cigar that is too wet is tough to draw as well; dried-out cigars can burn like wildfire.

Draw problems can often be solved during selection. Try to pick cigars that feel firm to the touch but not overly packed or hard. Cigars that feel soft and squishy can be underfilled, but may turn into a nice smoke as they burn down.

The completed cigars are then taken to special rooms, called marrying rooms, where they will undergo the final step in their manufacture. Here, their various components will marry, or blend, yielding the unique characteristics of their particular brand. These aging rooms, constructed of Spanish cedar and carefully temperature controlled, also help balance the humidity levels of the cigars, which must now dry out a little from the manufacturing process in order to yield a satisfying smoke. After aging, the cigars are again inspected and sorted by color of their wrappers. Since the wrapper is often the first thing that lures a smoker to a particular cigar, consistency in wrapper color is greatly desired. Some variation between wrappers is inevitable, however, and it is the sorter's responsibility to group cigars within a certain color range together so that when each box is opened at its final destination, the cigars inside look as even and consistent as possible. Finally, the cigars are banded.

HANDMADE VS. MACHINE-MADE

Machine-made cigars differ from handmade in several ways. The primary distinction between the two is the filler used to make them. Most, but not all, machine-made cigars are made with filler that consists of chopped-up pieces of tobacco. Their wrapper quality is often also somewhat less than what you'll find on premium hand-made cigars: usually coarser, possibly with protruding veins. The heads on machine-made cigars are often very pointed. If it doesn't have a cap, you can be certain your cigar is machine-made. If, when you remove it from its packaging, the head is either pierced or cut, it's a sure bet that a machine was used somewhere in its production.

Some cigars are now manufactured using a combination of hand and machine processes. Often, the filler and binder is bunched by machine, and a cigar roller affixes the wrapper and cap by hand. Cigars made in this fashion are often labeled as hand-rolled, but don't be fooled. They may have long filler and pretty decent wrappers, but they're not handmade, and the distinctions between them and premium handmade cigars will become apparent when you light one.

Machine-made and hand-rolled cigars aren't necessarily products to be avoided. Some of them are actually quite good and a good value as well. Machines are also used to manufacture many popular dry cigars, such as those made by Villiger, Schimmelpenninck, and Agio. They are also used to produce such cigars as the Muniemaker, a very decent machine-made cigar manufactured by F. D. Grave & Son in Pennsylvania, using Connecticut broadleaf for its wrapper and binder and a blend of domestic and imported tobacco for its filler.

Mass-market, machine-made cigars, on the other hand, are quite a different matter. Cigars that fall into this category include the ones you'll find at your local drug store or supermarket. They're usually made with something called homogenized tobacco leaf (HTL), an artificial product composed of bits and pieces of tobacco combined with water and other substances such as saltpeter and propylene glycol. Because of their manufacturing process, they are very consistent and they often yield a very mild smoke for those who prefer it. However, they're a far cry from a premium cigar, and very much removed from many machine-made ones as well.

HOW THEY'RE PACKAGED

Centuries ago, cigars were sold in bundles covered with pig bladders, with a pod or two of vanilla added to improve the smell. Thankfully, things have changed.

Why do some cigars taste like they've been dipped in something sweet?

Because they have been. Some cigars, such as the Arango Sportsman, pay homage to the storage methods of centuries ago and have been infused with vanilla, which makes them quite sweet. Also, some of the gums used to seal wrappers are slightly sweetened. Some people love it. Others hate it.

After pig bladders came large cedar chests, which were capable of holding up to 10,000 cigars. Cedar, of course, was used to keep the humidity level of the cigars stable, while helping to further the aging process.

The tradition of using smaller boxes began in 1830, when the banking firm of H. Upmann started shipping cigars manufactured in Cuba to its directors in London in sealed cedar boxes that were stamped with the bank's emblem. The bank eventually went full-scale into the cigar manufacturing business, and the cedar box took off as a form of packaging for all major Havana brands. Today, although many cigars still come packaged in cedar boxes, cardboard and other types of wood, especially mahogany, are also being used due to the increasing rarity and rising costs of cedar.

I like to leave the band on my cigar; my boyfriend always removes his. Which way is correct?

Smoking a dressed or undressed cigar is definitely a personal preference, and there's really no one correct way. For me, a great deal of the joy of smoking has to do with the way the cigar looks and feels, and the band completes the picture. I usually don't take them off until I have to, which is when the band starts to interfere with the formation of the ash (if I'm smoking my current selection down pretty far). Some cigars come with a band at their foot rather than near the head. Obviously, this is removed prior to lighting the cigar.

If you want to remove the band, wait until you've smoked the cigar a little bit. The heat from the cigar will loosen the glue of the band just enough to help it slip off easily. If you can't get the band off easily, don't force it, because you might tear the wrapper in so doing.

Boxes that are decorated with labels and decorative bands around their edges are called dress boxes; cabinet boxes are left fairly free of labels. Cigar boxes can hold various amounts of cigars, depending on their size and the size of the cigars; a fairly standard count is twenty-five.

You'll often find a colored ribbon under one of the cigars on the top layer of a box. Pull up on this ribbon, and you'll find that its purpose is to help you remove it and its neighbors from the box. Sometimes the layers will be divided by cedar or other packaging materials such as paper or thin cardboard. Some cigars are wrapped in cellophane, which some manufacturers feel better protects them when they're shipped. Others are packaged in special tubes or other wrappings to help maintain their humidity levels.

Now that you've explored how cigars are made and learned their anatomy and how they're packaged, it's time for your next step. It's time to enter the humidor.

3

Selecting Your Cigar

A man's shoes will tell you if he has money.
His clothes if he has style. But if you want to know
if he's a sport, see if he is wearing a good cigar.

Nat Sherman

I love smoking cigars, but I enjoy the ritual of buying them even
more. Each visit to a tobacconist is an adventure, every entry into
the humidor a highly anticipated treat. I always hope I'll find some
of my old favorites resting on their usual shelves. But there's always
the chance that I'll discover something new and wonderful to try as
well.

America's long-time affection for tobacco means there's a tobacconist in just about every city of any size in this country, and the
cigar's newfound popularity also means that there are more well-
equipped humidors and specialty cigar stores around than ever before.

FINDING CIGARS

Finding cigars? Surely, this can't be difficult, you might be thinking.
But it can be. If you've never smoked premium tobacco products,
you may never have had a reason to pay attention to where tobacconists or cigar shops are located. Check your local telephone direc-

tory under tobacco, cigars, or magazines. Yes, magazines. Many magazine shops or newsstands also feature a good selection of premium cigars, and they may even have walk-in humidors. Liquor stores, especially larger ones, are also a place to look, as more of them are adding or expanding their cigar inventory as a convenience to their customers. If you're on-line, try checking for recommendations there.

I can't find my favorite cigars at any local tobacconist. My friend says it's time to investigate ordering them over the phone, as he's done this often in the past with good success. Your thoughts?

Absolutely, give it a try. There's nothing wrong with ordering cigars from other sources than your local tobacconist, and it's even a good idea to develop contacts and resources in other parts of the country if you're searching for certain cigars that always seem to be in short supply where you live.

If your friend has suppliers he's dealt with successfully in the past, start with these sources. There's also a number of places to buy cigars from on the Internet.

Cigars are also available through mail order, and there's certainly some advantages to buying them this way. However, most of them don't apply to beginning cigar smokers. If you're just starting to smoke cigars, it's important to try a number of them to determine your smoking preferences. This is possible when you're buying locally, as tobacconists usually sell their cigars either singly or by the box. Mail-order houses will usually require you to buy cigars by the box, which is fine if you know exactly what you want. It's not so great if you get stuck with a box of cigars that you really don't like. There is also a great deal to be said for establishing a relationship with your local tobacconist. Not only are you supporting your local economy, you're also gaining the experience and advice of someone who will most likely know a great deal more about cigars than you do, and who will, hopefully, work with you as you develop your smoking preferences. However, not everyone is fortunate enough to live near a tobacconist or cigar shop. If that's the case, purchasing through mail order might be a necessity.

If you live in an area with more than one tobacconist nearby, by all means visit each one. Although you can expect to find basic similarities among all tobacconists, each store will have its own ambiance and its own selection. You'll definitely like some better than others.

Like many cigar smokers, I prefer a humidor I can walk into, and this preference greatly determines my choice of tobacco shops. Not only do I derive immense enjoyment from strolling about these special rooms, I think they also do a better job of storing cigars than case humidors, which can let in too much light and let out too much balanced air each time they are opened. However, some of the bigger and better stores in the United States often have a combination of both, so don't let case humidors deter you if the cigars appear to be in good shape. Never buy cigars from a box left out open in a store—they're bound to be dry and in need of rehumidifying.

HUMIDOR ETIQUETTE

Humidors are much like very special and specially equipped rooms in private homes. Although you are a customer, you are also a guest of the tobacconist when you enter one, and you should treat your time in there as such. Here are a few rules of order to keep in mind prior to entering your first humidor (guaranteed to make you a favored customer at any tobacconist's shop):

1. *Never smoke in a humidor room.* These rooms, due to the way they're constructed and the methods employed to maintain their temperature and humidity, do not dissipate aromas quickly, meaning that a brief puff of smoke will languish and linger in the air for many days. If enough people do it, the residue from the smoke will also clog the filtration and cir-

culation system with which the room is equipped. Also keep in mind that if these rooms don't dissipate the smell of smoke very quickly, they also will retain other scents for a very long time (if you catch my drift). Don't do anything in a humidor room that may cause you to be embarrassed when the next person walks into the room. This also goes for wearing strong perfumes and colognes.

2. *Handle the merchandise gently.* There's a right way and a wrong way to judge a cigar by hand, which we'll go into in greater detail later. For now, just keep in mind that cigars are fairly delicate things and don't stand up well to being pawed at, squished, or dropped. For these reasons, it's a good idea to keep young children out of humidor rooms. Not only is it difficult to select cigars when you're trying to keep an eye on Junior, the excitement caused by looking at all those cigars can be disruptive for other humidor customers. To young eyes, looking at all those cigars is as much fun as going to the dime store. The grab complex definitely comes out!

3. *Park your animals outside.* It's difficult to overcome the sudden urge to buy a cigar when you pass your favorite tobacconist while out on a leisurely stroll with your dog (I find it difficult myself), but unless you're a very good customer, most tobacconists would prefer you park your pooch somewhere else than in their store. Not long ago, a particularly good customer at my local tobacconist had forgotten his leash at home, and he assured the store staff that his pup would behave if allowed to enter the humidor. Well, you guessed it. No sooner had he set down poochie than the little guy created his own cigar on the floor. Definitely a mess, and a problem that related back to the first point (sadly enough). Not the sort of aroma you'd want in your humidor at any time!

A friend of mine loves to go into great detail when describing how his favorite cigars taste. To me, they either taste pretty good or pretty awful. Are his taste buds more developed or refined than mine, or am I just not getting it?

This question raises the age-old debate about cigars and the way they taste. And there's really no right or wrong answer. Everyone is constructed differently, we all have different taste buds, and we all perceive the way things taste in a different way.

I think the people who can dissect the way a cigar tastes from start to finish are probably the same people who can whiff at a cup of coffee and tell you the blend, where the beans were harvested, how they were roasted and when; or, when they drink wine, know down to the nth degree the vintage and the genesis of that wine just by taking a sip. And that's fine. But I can't do it, nor would I really want to spend the time developing the capacity to do it. For me, cigars tend to fall into two categories: those I like and those I don't. I can roughly describe the taste of some of them as peanutty, chocolately, buttery, tasting of coffee, cedary, salty, spicy, peppery, etc. Beyond that, I really can't identify specific spices or flavors. And then there are some that I just like because they have a good blend of tobacco and they burn well.

The best advice is not to worry about whether or not you can describe how a cigar tastes. Just enjoy them!

4. *Don't offer your advice to other humidor customers unless you're quite sure it's welcome.* Nothing burns my butt faster (and the butts of other humidor customers) than the cigar snob or boor who hangs out in a humidor room, loudly offering his (and sometimes her) pearls of wisdom about the best cigar he/she's ever smoked (which the tobacconist usually won't have) to anyone unlucky enough to spend a few minutes in the proximate area. Most of us are too polite to tell you to shut up and leave, but if you notice that everyone pretty

much wants to ignore you when you're regaling us with your advice, it's a good idea for you to zip it or motor out on your own steam.

5. *Be courteous to the humidor room staff.* They're there to help you. Sometimes they may not be able to fully anticipate your needs, and you need to help them by telling them what you're searching for, or maybe recalling something that you've liked in the past. If you truly don't want their help, politely decline it. But don't hesitate to speak up if there's something you need or something you can't find.

6. *Don't bellyache about the prices to humidor staff or salespeople.* It isn't their fault. If you truly have a concern, ask to speak to the manager or owner.

7. *If a method is provided to help you keep track of prices, consider using it.* Many tobacconists make available small clipboards with pads of paper and pens or pencils so that customers making multiple selections can keep track of their prices. Not only does this speed up your visit to the cash register, it also can serve as a good reference tool if you're just starting out and want to keep track of prices at various tobacconists. The large assortment of cigars (and the new brands arriving almost every month) make it difficult for sales staff to remember all the prices in their humidors. Everyone appreciates considerate customers who will help in this area.

8. *Remember to close the door behind you when entering and exiting the humidor.* This may sound obvious and picky, but you'd be surprised how many people don't do this. Leaving the door open causes excessive strain on the devices used to maintain the atmosphere in the humidor, and, obviously, defeats the purpose of the humidor in the first place.

9. *If you see a problem in the humidor, don't hesitate to point it out to the humidor attendant or sales staff.* It's difficult to mon-

itor the condition of thousands of cigars when visited daily by dozens of customers. Although any good tobacconist devotes a substantial portion of his or her time to properly maintaining a humidor and its contents, it's still possible to miss a cigar with a cracked wrapper or one sporting a mold spot or two (it does happen, even in the best humidors). Let them know, discreetly, if possible.

10. *If the humidor you're visiting is in the United States, don't ask if they have Cuban cigars.* They don't.

INTO THE HUMIDOR

Now that you have an idea of how you should act when visiting a humidor, it's time to actually enter one and choose your cigar (or cigars).

On your first visit to a walk-in humidor, spend a few moments just getting used to the environment. If it's cold outside and you're wearing glasses, be prepared to wipe the condensation off your lenses or wait for them to clear, as the humidor room will be warmer and more humid than the atmosphere you've just left. Let your eyes adjust to the light in the humidor, which is usually somewhat more subdued (at least, it should be) than the lighting in the other parts of the store.

Humidors are generally constructed with wood shelves, either flat or slanting, which display cigars in open boxes. How they're organized will vary from tobacconist to tobacconist, and there may not seem to be much rhyme or reason to it (and, frankly, there probably isn't in most stores). You'll see Dominican cigars next to Honduran, and Honduran next to Nicaraguan; however, different sizes and styles of cigars within the same brand are almost always displayed together.

With so many different brands and styles of cigars to choose from, just viewing the variety displayed on the shelves can be overwhelming if you're just starting your cigar smoking experience. So, where to begin?

I'm ready to buy my first box of cigars. How should I go about doing it?

If you're thinking about buying an unopened box, have your tobacconist open the box so you can check the contents. In general, the cigars should look good and be of the same color. Feel one or two of them to make sure they're healthy. If they crackle when you're doing this, they've been around for awhile and may be dry. If you want, go ahead and give the cigars a good sniff to see if you like their bouquet. They should smell great if the box is freshly opened. Most tobacconists won't mind you smelling the cigars at this point if you're serious about buying them.

One way to attack a humidor is to search out a specific brand, if you have one in mind. If there's a humidor attendant available, ask if your intended brand is in stock. If it is, great, you're set, and you can make your selection and end your transaction here or search out another brand, similar or not. If it's not, ask the attendant for a recommendation. He or she will usually ask you a few questions, such as what you may have smoked before, the strength of cigar you prefer, whether you like a spicy or smooth smoke, your wrapper preference, etc. The more information you can give humidor attendants, the easier it is for them to make good recommendations. However, if you are truly clueless, don't worry. They'll help you find something you like.

I just bought a box of cigars from my favorite tobacconist, only to find the first one absolutely unsmokable! I don't want to waste my time or my money on them. Is there a remedy?

It depends on your definition of unsmokable. If there's something wrong with the cigars that has affected their quality, if they haven't been stored correctly, for example, by all means take the box back to your tobacconist and discuss the problem. Any good tobacconist will want to work with you to solve the problem, especially if you're a good customer.

If the cigars just don't meet up to your expectations, chances are you can still return them if you've stored them properly. Most likely you'll get a store credit for future purchases.

THE OUTSIDE OF THE CIGAR

Spend a few minutes just looking at the various cigars if you don't have a specific brand in mind. Note the different sizes and the wide variety of wrapper colors. Ranging from light green to a brown so dark they appear to be black, cigar wrappers are the strong visual cue that lures us to one cigar over another. Although there are eight basic wrapper colors, you'll find variations within each category, and, sometimes, between manufacturers, as what will be a Colorado claro to one might just be a plain old claro to another. It can be a bit confusing, but the distinctions below should help you tell the difference between a maduro and a natural.

Double Claro

Also called Candela or American Market Select, these cigars are the lightest of the light, ranging from a very light green to greenish brown. The color is achieved by picking the leaf before it reaches maturity and then drying it rapidly by heating it, which allows greater control over its final color. This is a very mild, bland wrapper with very little oil. For a long time, it was the favored wrapper for cigars targeted for the U.S. market, hence its name. You won't see it too often today.

Claro

This shade-grown tobacco is usually light tan, so anything marked as having a Connecticut shade wrapper will most likely be claro in color. These wrappers generally have neutral flavor and are very smooth to smoke. Think of a cup of tea with lots of milk in it, and you have the color of a claro wrapper.

Natural

Natural wrappers are also called English Market Select, and range in color from medium tan to brown. Natural wrappers can really run the gamut when it comes to their color, so don't be put off if a box of cigars marked EMS looks pretty dark. They're most often sun-grown, which contributes to their stronger color and fuller flavor, and there's often more oil present on their surface. They're still very smooth to smoke.

Colorado Claro

The Colorado claro is a medium brown, tawny-colored wrapper. Think of it as a natural wrapper with a reddish tint. Wrappers grown in Cameroon often sport this color. They're often on the spicy side.

Colorado

A cigar with this reddish dark brown, aromatic wrapper tastes robust and rich.

Colorado Maduro

This wrapper is dark brown, medium strength, and slightly more aromatic than the maduro. It usually gives a rich flavor, as found in many of the best Honduran cigars.

Maduro

These dark brown to very dark brown wrappers usually have more texture and veining than the lighter wrappers because it takes a heavier leaf to stand up to the curing process required to turn maduro wrappers their darker color. They are often described as oily-looking, with a stronger taste—sweet to some palates—and a unique aroma.

Oscuro

Very dark brown or almost black, they are the strongest-tasting of all wrappers. These wrappers tend to be from Nicaragua, Brazil, Mexico, or Connecticut broadleaf (as opposed to the shade).

In general, the darker the wrapper color, the stronger and sweeter its flavor is likely to be. Darker wrappers usually spend a longer time on their host plant or they come from higher altitudes (the extra exposure to sunlight produces more oil as well as sugar, both of which make wrappers darker and fuller-tasting). They also will have undergone a longer fermentation process.

Another method of choosing a cigar is to search for cigars that feature tobaccos from a specific country. Since there are differences in the soil from country to country, tobacco grown in a certain country takes on distinct properties and the cigars made from those tobaccos will be similar as well.

WHERE TOBACCO IS GROWN

Brazil

Two regions of this South American country produce medium to full-bodied tobacco that is used for both humidified and non-humidified or dry cigars.

Cameroon

Originally just grown in this West African country, Cameroon seed is now sown in other countries as well. It is very flavorful, with an aroma that can border on being pungent. Many cigar smokers show a strong preference for Cameroon wrappers.

Cuba

Cuba's legendary soil produces cigars that are capable of making grown men (and women) weep and beg for more. Of the island's four growing regions, the best-known is the Vuelta Abajo region located on the west side of the island, which produces an exquisite shade-grown wrapper as well as filler tobacco. Although cigars with Cuban tobacco are often thought to be heavy, they can also be surprisingly mild—at least in comparison with other Cuban cigars. What is always consistent about Cuban cigars is that they have a flavor like none other.

Dominican Republic

This island country (it's just to the right of Haiti) produces the majority of the world's premium cigars. Most noted for its long-leaf filler, the Dominican Republic also recently began producing wrapper tobacco, following years of experimentation with various combinations of soil and seed. Tobacco from this country ranks as mild to mild-medium.

Ecuador

An almost perpetual cloud cover here creates natural shade-grown wrappers with a mild, yet flavorful taste.

Honduras

This Central American country is ranked as the second-largest producer of non-Havana premium cigars in the world. Honduran tobacco tends to be rich and somewhat spicy.

Jamaica

One of the countries chosen by Cubans fleeing the country following the revolution of 1898, Jamaica produces a somewhat mild yet flavorful tobacco.

Mexico

Mexico has several tobacco-growing regions that produce binder, filler, and wrapper tobacco. Mexican tobacco can be either extremely mild or rough and harsh; it always has a certain flavor that distinguishes it from tobacco grown in other countries. It produces a lot of binder leaf and is noted for its somewhat spicy maduro wrappers.

Nicaragua

Located just south of Honduras, Nicaragua has weathered its share of problems over the years, both natural and man-made, making its tobacco and cigar producing efforts uneven at times. When things are good, this country can produce some great cigars with medium body and often a somewhat sweet taste.

Sumatra

Sumatra, along with neighboring Java, produces a wrapper leaf used for both humidified and nonhumidified cigars. They are mild, but with some spice.

United States

The United States is primarily noted for the shade and broadleaf wrapper from the Connecticut Valley. This flavorful wrapper is always very much in demand, which drives up the price of any cigar using it.

In general, cigars made with tobacco from Jamaica or the Philippines tend to be the mildest, the Dominican Republic produces cigars mild to medium in strength, and cigars from Honduras and Nicaragua are stronger and heavier. However, within these general categories you'll also find differences between brands, depending on the blend of the tobacco in the filler, how (and for how long) the tobacco was cured, the type of wrapper used, and how the cigar itself was rolled.

Another factor to keep in mind when selecting your cigar is the size and shape you wish to smoke. Feel free to choose whatever style appeals to you (forget anything you've ever heard about the necessity of choosing a cigar to complement the size and shape of your body), but keep in mind that length and circumference—in cigars, referred to as ring size—will greatly determine the way a cigar will taste and smoke. (Ring size, by the way, is measured in 1/64th of an inch increments. If a cigar has a ring size of 45, it is 45/64ths of an inch thick. Cigars with ring sizes of 50 and above are nearing an inch thick.) In general, cigars with bigger ring sizes deliver a fuller taste. Long, thin cigars are generally made with less variety of tobaccos in their filler because it's difficult to get more than one or two into a skinny cigar. They'll generally be a less intense smoke than the same brand of cigar in a bigger ring size. Longer cigars may smoke a bit cooler than shorter ones, but in general, length is a greater determinant of smoking time than anything else.

CIGAR SIZES

Ranging from the slimmest, smallest cigarillo to the largest double corona, there truly is a cigar made to suit every smoking preference and occasion. In the past, certain cigar shape names such as Churchill or corona had specific meanings in the cigar industry; today, however, what these shape names signify can vary a great deal from one manufacturer to another. Confusing? Absolutely!

Perelman's Pocket Cyclopedia of Cigars lists no less than twenty well-known cigar shapes, and if you want to get very picky about knowing the exact designation for the cigar you're smoking, it's the place to look. If you just want the basics, the following descriptions should give you an idea of some standard sizes, as well as their measurements and their smoking time.

Cigarillo
The smallest of the small, they usually measure no longer than 6 inches and no bigger around than 29 ring (most are substantially smaller than this). Often machine-made, these mini cigars provide a quick smoke (ten minutes or so) that most find preferable to cigarettes.

Panatela

Long and narrow, these cigars can range from 7 inches long to as short as 4 or 5 inches. Their ring size is never bigger than a 39, and you'll see them as thin as 30. Smoking time will be twenty to thirty minutes, depending on length.

Corona/Petit Corona

Shorter and stubbier than a panatela, these cigars can pack a lot of smoking pleasure into a pretty small size. They start at 4 inches and range up to almost 6 inches, with ring sizes ranging from 40 to 44. These are a great choice for a fuller, albeit quick smoke, of about thirty to forty minutes.

Long Corona/Lonsdale

These cigars start at about 6 inches and range up to just past 7 inches, with ring sizes in the 40 to 44 range. The Lonsdale, by the way, was named for the Earl of Lonsdale, who in the early 1900s commissioned a cigar factory in Havana to produce his own cigars of a distinctive length and shape, and then had them packed into boxes bearing his portrait. Smoking time is forty-five minutes to an hour.

Giant/Grand Corona

These are longer than a long corona, but still on the narrow ring size side, with lengths ranging from 6½ inches to over 7½ and gauges of 42 to 47. Smoking time is forty-five minutes to an hour here as well.

Robusto/Toro

Short and squatty, these cigars pack lots of smoking wallop into a very small package. They look like a Churchill chopped in half, and today they're very popular because they can deliver all the fullness and flavor of their longer cousins in half the smoking time. They range from 5 inches to just over 6½, with ring sizes running from 48 to 54. The term *robusto* is fairly new in describing these cigars; you'll also see them with the older designation

Rothschild, so named for London financier Leopold de Rothschild, for whom they were originally created by the Hoyo de Monterrey factory in Cuba. Rothschild wanted a short cigar with a large ring size so he could enjoy the richest flavor possible without having to take the time to smoke a full-length cigar. They provide about an hour of smoking pleasure.

Churchill/Double Corona

These cigars are the longest and the fattest, although the classic Churchill actually has a fairly narrow ring size at 47. Ranging from 7 inches on up, these are the kings of cigars. You'll find them with ring sizes ranging from 46 to 54. Plan on spending more than an hour smoking them.

Shaped Cigars

These cigars differ from the others in that their sides are not exactly straight from top to bottom. *Pyramids* increase continuously from head to foot. *Torpedos* or *diademases* start with shaped heads and gradually grow to large ring sizes near the foot, where they taper rapidly into closed feet. *Belicosos* have tapered heads that immediately flare out to straight sides running the entire length of the cigar. *Perfectos,* which resemble torpedos, start with a rounded head and end with a closed foot. They are often constructed with a more pronounced bulge in the middle than torpedos, and can vary significantly in length. Rarely seen is the *culebra,* which consists of three small cigars twisted together (and smoked separately).

Most of the cigars you'll see displayed will be straight-sided, meaning they have the same ring size from head to foot. When you're just starting out, spend your money and your time getting to know these cigars before moving on to figurados or shaped cigars. These cigars, with their varying ring sizes, are usually shaped by hand since they won't fit into cigar forms. Because of this, they're more expensive. The differences in the way some of these cigars smoke, while of interest to experienced cigar smokers, are somewhat wasted on new cigar smokers.

When you've finally arrived at the cigar of your choice, select one from its box and examine it. Handling it by its foot—usually the end that is cut—is the courteous thing to do, as the head, or the closed end, is the part that will go into your mouth—or someone else's. The first thing you should note is its weight. Although a cigar generally isn't very heavy, its weight should be appropriate to its size. A large cigar that feels light may be underfilled or dry; a heavy-feeling robusto may be too tightly rolled for you to enjoy it.

Why do some cigars come with cellophane, and some do not, and when should I remove the cellophane from the ones that do have it?

It is thought by many manufacturers that wrapping cigars in cellophane helps protect the cigar from the date it is shipped to the second it arrives in your fingers.

Removing the cellophane is a subject of much discourse among cigar smokers. If you're buying just a few cigars, leave the cellophane on until you smoke them. It will help keep the cigar moist, but by no means will it preserve the cigar in the condition it should be. You should still store the cigars appropriately.

Don't, as I've seen some people do, cut your cigar through the cellophane. If you're cutting in anticipation of smoking, there's no reason to keep the cellophane on that cigar. And, since you're removing the top when you trim it, the cellophane isn't going to do much of a job of keeping your cigar fresh. If you're in a shop and you want the cigars cut, the tobacconist should remove the cellophane, trim the heads, and place all your purchases in a plastic bag to preserve them. Trying to reinsert them into the cellophane, as I've also seen people try to do (some with better success than others), might damage fragile cigar wrappers.

Take a good look at how it's constructed. You want to see an evenly rolled wrapper, with no cracks along its body. (It's not uncommon, however, to see a few wrapper cracks at the foot of a noncellophaned cigar. They'll rarely affect the way the cigar will smoke.) If you find a cigar that is beginning to unravel, put it aside or point it out to the tobacconist and select another one.

The color of the wrapper should be even as well, although a few sun spots, again, will not affect the way the cigar will taste or smoke. Occasionally, you might see a small patch in the body of a cigar; this is done to repair a hole in an otherwise good wrapper leaf and won't affect the way the cigar will smoke.

The last part of your inspection consists of feeling the cigar, which you should do very gently, from head to foot. A well-made, well-humidified cigar will have a consistent feel from top to bottom with no significant hard or soft spots, which may indicate problems with the way the cigar was bunched or stored. How hard or soft the cigar will feel overall will vary somewhat from brand to brand, as each manufacturer has its own method of fashioning its cigars. In general, what you're looking for is a cigar that feels healthy to the touch. This is possible to discern even through cellophane wrappers. It is not necessary to remove the cellophane from any cigar you're considering, and you should not do it unless you're intending on buying that exact cigar. Obviously, the same holds true for cigars encased in tubes or humidor packs, which are opaque coverings, heavier than cellophane, used by some manufacturers. Never open them! If you're interested in buying a tubed or wrapped cigar, ask the tobacconist for the characteristics of that particular cigar.

You may see humidor customers roll cigars in their fingertips by their ears. What they're doing is something called listening to the band, which they think is an indication of the health of the cigar. What they're actually doing is stressing an already fragile wrapper, and this practice causes more wrapper cracks in humidors than anything else. It's not necessary to roll a cigar in your fingers to judge its state. Merely giving it a gentle feel will tell you everything you need to know.

Another thing you'll see people do is smell their cigars. Although I'm guilty of doing this as well, since I love the way cigars smell, it really isn't necessary when deciding what cigar is right for you. It also isn't the most sanitary practice I can think of. Remember, the cigar that's now in your hand may have been felt and sniffed by many other people, some of whom, most assuredly, aren't as fastidious about their hygiene as you are. As a general rule, only put a cigar to your nostrils if you're going to buy it.

Some cigars come in a metal or glass storage tube or are wrapped in what my tobacconist calls a humidor pack. How long will these devices keep a cigar fresh?

Although these devices are often thought to be airtight, they aren't. Don't keep a cigar protected in metal or glass tubes outside of a humidor or other humidifying device for more than a day or two at the most. Cigars in humidor packs can last longer. Resist opening the packaging to smell them, too, as you will let in dry air that will affect them.

Once you've made your selections, take them to the cash register and pay for them. Most tobacconists will offer to place your purchases in a plastic bag, and they'll be fine for a couple of days or so in that bag if you keep it sealed. The tobacconist may ask you if you want any of your purchases cut, which means the head will be trimmed in preparation for smoking. If you do, you may ask the tobacconist to do it, or . . . proceed on to the next chapter!

My tobacconist often offers to cut the head of a cigar for me before I leave the shop. Is this proper?

Sure, but it doesn't necessarily mean he or she wants to do the actual cutting. They will, by all means, but a true cigar enthusiast will trim the head of his or her own cigar. However, if you have any concerns about your technique or want to see a new style of cutter demonstrated, by all means ask to have the head cut. Watch and learn.

You may see cigars at a tobacconist cellophaned together into a bundle. These are known as bundled cigars, and they can often represent a good smoking value because they cost less for the manufacturer to package. Some bundled cigars are seconds—cigars that failed the manufacturer's final inspection for various reasons, usually because they had uneven wrapper colors or blemishes, they have uneven sides, or they may not have been cut straight when they were sized. However, some companies now make cigars specifically for packaging into bundles.

Obviously, judging the characteristics of bundled cigars can be difficult. If you're interested in purchasing cigars packaged in this fashion, ask your tobacconist for his or her recommendations.

KEEPING TRACK

As you expand your cigar experience, you may enjoy keeping track of your choices, much like wine lovers keep records of their favorite vintages.

An easy way to do this is in a small three-ring notebook. Keep it near where you smoke most often so you can make notes while you smoke. Consider buying a notebook with at least one pocket so you can store such things as a ring gauge guide, ruler, and any cigar bands you haven't yet glued down on paper. Alphabetical dividers are nice but not essential. If you want to get really fancy, you can record your cigar-smoking experiences in a very elegant bound book called the *Cigar Dossier*; it's available through tobacconists or bookstores.

The basic things to list include the name and style of the cigar, the date it was smoked (and maybe the time), when and where it was purchased, and how much you paid. Many people, myself included, also like to paste in the cigar band as a visual reference to the cigar we're describing. Other things to note include the cigar's aroma both before and during smoking, its construction, strength and taste, wrapper style, and how it smoked and burned. If you keep track of ring sizes, lengths, and countries of manufacture as well, you'll eventually see a pattern to your cigar smoking that can greatly assist your selection process in the humidor.

4

Rites and Rituals

There are more ways than one to do anything...

G. CABRERA INFANTE, *HOLY SMOKE*

Much, perhaps too much, has been written about the correct ways in which cigars should be cut and lit; most of it, I think, only serves to confuse and daunt beginning cigar smokers. Certainly, there are some basics to keep in mind, but I tend to agree with my good friend Pinkster, a long-time smoker who has enjoyed more cigars than most of us will ever dream of, who, after graciously

---

I have a friend who makes a great show of smelling the cellophane when he removes it from his cigars. He swears it's as good an indication of a good cigar as smelling the cork from a bottle of wine is. Your thoughts?

What does he do when he smokes a cigar with no cellophane? Seriously, the way cellophane might smell (if it has any smell at all) has as little to do with the cigar once it's unwrapped as a cork once removed from a bottle of wine. Ask any wine expert, and they'll tell you the proper thing to do with a cork if it's presented to you to inspect once it's removed from a wine bottle is to feel it to make sure it isn't dry. Smelling it or the cellophane removed from a cigar will tell you nothing about either commodity.

---

demonstrating cutting and lighting to beginning cigar enthusiasts, always finishes his ministrations by growling, "Just get the damn thing lit."

That's the basic idea. Here's how to go about it.

HOW TO CUT A CIGAR (AND WHY)

Most premium handmade cigars are made with at least one capped end, sometimes two. The end that you'll draw smoke through—the head—must be cut or pierced in some way prior to lighting. The goal is to create an appropriately sized, clean opening that will allow the proper amount of smoke to be drawn through your cigar. Basically, what you're doing is creating a chimney above a fire, and an opening for the smoke to travel through. There are several different ways to do this, and a variety of different tools you can use.

Is there one correct way? Not really, although several are preferred. Many smokers use a combination of cutting methods, depending on the situation and tools at hand.

Off With Its Head!—Guillotine Cutters
Perhaps the most popular cutting style today is the guillotine, which, as its name implies, lops the head off the cigar, leaving a straight, open, circular end. This cut provides a large surface for the smoke to pass through, which helps prevent excessive buildup of residue and smoke in the head of the cigar.

Guillotine cutters, by far the most popular cutters used today, are available in both single and double blade versions. One of the best is a single blade version marketed by cigar aficionado Paul Garmarian. It's sleek, absolutely razor sharp, and comes in a closable carrying case so it can be tossed into a pocket or purse without fear of dinging it up. Another very popular, very good guillotine-style cutter is the Zino by Zino Davidoff. It's a double-blade cutter, preferred by many people because it applies pressure to the cigar from both sides as it cuts. Plan to spend around $55 and up for either of these cutters.

Other, less expensive guillotine cutters are also available at almost any tobacconist. As you go down in price, you'll notice definite differences in quality of both the case and the cutting blade. The least expensive cutters will be housed in very cheap plastic and may have blades that will actually bend as you try to cut your cigar, which, while not causing serious problems, does create interesting convex or concave cuts when you're striving for a straight cut.

Let price be your guide when selecting a guillotine cutter, but keep in mind that you'll end up replacing a cheap one more frequently than you'd like, and they usually break at the most inopportune times (like at special occasions and when every tobacconist in the city is closed). Some folks would rather buy a whole lot of $2.50 cutters than one $55 one. I'm not one of them.

Help! My cigar is coming unraveled!

This rarely happens, but the sad fact is that there's little you can do if your wrapper is actually unraveling. It's usually due to faulty or insufficient gum used to seal the wrapper once it's done being rolled, compounded by less-than-optimal storage conditions, either yours or the tobacconists'. Once a cigar truly starts to unravel, it will usually keep going at one level or another until the whole thing is undone, and all that you have left on your hands is a smoking, burning mess. Get rid of it.

When making a guillotine cut, only the very top of the cigar is inserted into the cutter. Do not insert the cigar all the way down to the end of the cap or lop off the entire first inch of the cigar as I've seen some smokers do. The goal is to only remove as much of the cap as necessary to give you a good burn and even draw—usually about 1/16th of an inch or so. Not only does cutting the entire cap off (or more) run you the risk of unraveling the cigar, you're also unnecessarily wasting good tobacco.

Cigar scissors, which also yield a guillotine cut, provide a somewhat elegant means of trimming the head of a cigar. They're available in several sizes. I find the larger ones easier to manipulate, which limits their practicality for me (you won't catch me with a pair in my purse or pocket). Most cigar scissors come with some sort of a case or cover to protect the blades. Plan to spend at least $50 for a good pair; beautifully balanced scissors such as the ones available from Davidoff of Geneva will set you back at least $300 or more.

A guillotine cut can also be made with a small knife or scissors; in fact, the scissors included on many Swiss army knives are excellent cigar cutters. I've also used a small pair of fly-tying scissors in a pinch. Just make sure they're sharp for the best cut.

V FOR VICTORY

An older-style cut, but still favored by some cigar smokers is the V cut, also called a cat-eye cut, which makes a V-shaped notch in the head of the cigar. (For the obvious reason, it is said to have been Churchill's favorite.) You'll sometimes see machine-made cigars finished with this cut, which does make them a handy smoke. Advocates of the V cut will tell you this cut produces enough surface area for drawing smoke through, while keeping the cut surface of the tobacco away from the mouth.

You will need a special tool, called a V cutter, to facilitate this cut. This is a device with a long handle, topped with a two-piece cutter (in some respects, it's pretty versatile, as the handle can be used to open a sealed box of cigars and it even sports a small groove that you can use to remove the nail from the box top). You insert the head of the cigar into the bottom opening of the cutter and press down on the top piece. It plunges down into the bottom, taking a V-shaped notch out of the top of the cigar.

Most V cutters I've had my hands on won't accommodate the larger ring styles popular today, yielding too shallow a cut. This cutting style can cut too deeply into the cap of a smaller-gauge cigar, in effect removing most of the cap and causing an eventual cave-in of the head. I also think it causes more bits and pieces of tobacco than a guillotine cut because it slices diagonally through the tobacco rather than straight across it. Frankly, I can't think of a good reason for this cut, but some people like to be contrarians. Plan to spend a minimum of $60 for a decent tabletop V cutter. Pocket models (minus the spring that makes the cutter a little easier to operate) are also available.

PLUCKING, PUNCHING, AND PIERCING

These are also older-style cutting methods. Neither makes much sense to me as they do not produce a broad surface on the head of the cigar, but again, you'll find people who are utterly devoted to them, and there are some smokers who prefer a more concentrated stream of smoke on their tongues, which these cutting styles definitely deliver.

Pluckers or punchers actually take a small punch out of the head of the cigar. It's up to you to decide how deep you want the punch to be. This style of cut is also known as the bird's-eye cut, since you end up with the end of your cigar looking somewhat like a tiny eyeball when you do it correctly.

A popular plucker, called the Magnum, looks just like a .44 Magnum bullet. You pull apart the bullet to reveal the cutting edge, which you then punch into the top of the cigar. Turn and pull gently to remove it, and a small piece of the cap will come out with it. Another plucker-style cutter incorporates a small plunger to facilitate the removal of the cap from the cutter.

Piercers are pinlike devices that you use to puncture the top of the cigar. This method used to be very popular, and, again, you'll find machine-made cigars manufactured with holes in their heads. Many smokers now feel that a small pierced opening compresses the filler of the cigar, creating an unpleasant, overheated smoke. In a pinch, you can use a bamboo skewer or poultry trussing pin to make this cut, if it's one you prefer.

Plucker and piercer cutters are usually relatively inexpensive, often in the $10 to $15 range, which I think governs their choice for many cigar smokers who would rather spend their money on cigars than on the devices used to cut them. They're also handy, convenient, and are often available in key-ring versions.

TRIMMING WITH YOUR TEETH

Yes, it works, but it's not very proper, and most people end up with little bits and pieces of tobacco stuck in their teeth and floating around their mouths. It also takes some practice to end up with a good, even cut rather than a smashed, uneven butt. Better than nothing in a pinch, but I'd still try to find a small knife instead. If you're using your teeth, try for the same kind of cut you'd effect with a guillotine—straight and even across the top. It tends to be most effective with cigars of a smaller ring size.

CHOOSING AN IGNITION SOURCE

Once your cigar is cut and you're done admiring it in every way that seems fitting to you, it's time to light it. This may seem like a simple proposition, but getting a cigar lit correctly so that it draws and burns at its best can take a little time to perfect.

It may be tempting to use whatever book of matches or lighter you have at hand to light your cigar. That's fine, and it probably won't affect the taste of the cigar that much, but anyone who's been smoking cigars for a while would advise putting a little more thought into your choice of igniting methods. What you don't want to use is an ignition source that will affect the cigar's flavor. Cheaper pocket lighters and most matches have a high sulfur content, which definitely can affect the flavor of a cigar (be sure to let the sulfur burn off for a second or two before lighting a cigar with your average matches).

The best choices are butane lighters and low-sulfur cedar matches. Both can be found at most tobacconists. At a minimum, plan to spend about $20 on a butane lighter with enough flame to adequately light a cigar. Fancy lighters, such as the ones from S. T. Dupont (easily identified by the unique *ping* the more expensive ones make as they're flipped open), and the classic designs from the venerable house of Dunhill can run you many hundreds, even thousands of dollars, and can almost be considered jewelry for their workmanship, beauty, and appearance. However, if you're like me and you tend to misplace lighters, they're not worth the agony if they disappear.

Other companies such as Savinelli, Colibri, and KGM offer a number of lighters specifically designed for lighting cigars. Some produce angled flames, which work well on both cigars and pipes. Others utilize either a double flame or dual-flame system that definitely make short work of lighting even the largest robusto.

Colibri makes several different lines of lighters for cigars, some of which feature an integrated cutter for the ultimate in convenience (the cutter blade is replaceable as well). Take a look at Colibri's Quantum series if you smoke a lot outdoors; these lighters use a forced flame system that maintains a reliable flame even in a breeze. Plan to spend about $100 and up for any of these lighters.

Let comfort, convenience, and price guide you when selecting a lighter. Whatever you choose should fit your hand comfortably, and you should find it easy to light. Lighters are manufactured with a variety of firing mechanisms. You'll find some easier to operate than others.

You may also see several devices looking like torches at your local tobacconist. One is called the cigar torch, and it looks very much like a miniature version of the acetylene torches used by ironworkers.

What's the best way to put out a cigar so it will taste good when it's relit?

The best way is to just let it go out naturally in an ashtray. Most cigars will die down within a few minutes or so. Don't stub out the bottom, as doing so will cause a buildup of smoke and residue.

Another lighter that's currently very popular is called the mini blow-torch. It wasn't specifically designed to be used with cigars, but it does a great job of lighting them (keep one handy as a windshield defroster or lock deicer, if you live where you need such things). Look to spend anywhere from about $55 and up for these lighters.

Be careful when using a blowtorch-type lighter, especially if you're using one to relight a partially smoked cigar. Their flames are significantly longer than the blue area that is visible to the eye, and it is very easy to singe or burn eyebrows, hairlines, mustaches, and the like. They can also get very hot, so handle with care.

I left my partially smoked cigar in my ashtray overnight. Can I relight it?

Sometimes relighting can make a cigar burn and taste poorly, especially if the natural oils in the tobacco have accumulated in the stub. Also, leaving a partially smoked cigar out overnight will dry it out. However, if it's a cigar you enjoyed, and there's enough left to make relighting it worthwhile, by all means give it a shot.

When you're ready to fire it up, knock any dead ash that might remain from the end, and blow gently through the cigar to dissipate any stale smoke left behind from before. If the wrapper burned unevenly from the last smoke, try trimming it even with the end of the cigar before you relight.

Another lighting method popular with some cigar smokers is using a cedar strip or spill, usually a thin piece of the cedar that comes in a cigar box. Like using cedar matches, this method burns cleanly and gives off a good, hot flame. However, carrying those small pieces of cedar with you isn't always convenient, and too large a piece of cedar may produce more of a fire than you can easily control. Lighting one outside in a breeze is next to impossible.

LIGHTING UP

On to the actual lighting process. Your goal when lighting a cigar is to create a good coal that will burn evenly. Start by holding the foot of your cigar near a lit match or lighter for several seconds, making sure to rotate the cigar so that all sides are evenly heated. What you're doing is priming the cigar so that it will more easily accept the flame when you actually light it. You want to make sure the end of the cigar is charred or toasted evenly over its entire surface, but just the very end, not the entire foot. If you've got black smoke extending up the foot of the cigar, you've succeeded in turning the wrapper in that area to charcoal, and you've definitely affected the taste of your cigar. Holding your cigar horizontally will help keep this from happening.

Then put the cigar to your lips and rotate the flame around the foot. Don't immerse your cigar in the flame; It should be about a half inch away from the end. Instead, draw the flame to the cigar. If you're using matches, be prepared to use several during this process. Soon you'll begin to see a blackened rim and the beginnings of a burning coal. Take a few good puffs to make sure everything is burning evenly, and you should have a nicely lit cigar. Once you have it lit, you can blow through the glowing end to make sure it's burning evenly. If not, go back and light the nonburning areas again.

Some smokers mouth or lick the head of the cigar before they light it. I've even seen a few smokers, primarily older ones, lick the entire length of the cigar up and down. I suppose there's nothing wrong with this, but I can't really see a reason for it, especially if the cigar has been stored correctly and is properly moistened to begin with. These are oftentimes the same individuals who spend more time chewing on the head of their cigars than smoking them, rendering this end a disgusting mass of spit and tobacco. Yuk!

Another habit among older cigar smokers is running a flame briefly along the length of the cigar prior to lighting. This was originally done to burn off the taste and fragrance of the gum used to seal some cigars many years ago. Flavorless gums are used to seal cigars today, eliminating the need to perform this ancient ritual.

ONCE IT'S BURNING

First off, sit back and enjoy your cigar! Note how it looks in your hand, how the foot is burning, if the ash is burning evenly. When first lighting a cigar, it's easy to miss a part. You want to be sure that the wrapper on your cigar will burn as evenly as possible, so don't hesitate to relight it.

What causes some wrappers to burn unevenly, with one side burning faster than the other?

Wrappers that burn unevenly—this is called tunneling—can be caused by a number of factors. Sometimes it's caused by construction; your cigar may have a soft spot in the area where it's burning faster. Sometimes it's caused by uneven lighting; make sure you get the foot of the cigar burning evenly when you light it. Sometimes it's caused by the way the cigar has been packaged or stored; it may have absorbed more humidity on one side than the other, causing an uneven burn. Finally, air currents can cause cigars to burn unevenly. Many smokers who walk outside with their cigars report uneven burns on their wrappers. In these cases, there's not much you can do.

If the cigar you're smoking either cores or tunnels, you can try letting it go out, trimming it, and relighting it. Sometimes this will cure the problem.

Hold your cigar lightly but firmly in your mouth as you draw on it. Don't clamp down on it. It's unnecessary, and causes strain on your jaw. Take good, even draws on your cigar. Fill your mouth with smoke. Hold it briefly, then let it out. If you're a cigarette smoker, either current or past, it may take you a little time to learn to smoke with your mouth rather than your lungs; if you're sputtering and coughing when you take in the smoke from your cigar, you're definitely inhaling. Cigars aren't meant to be inhaled, but I think most cigar smokers do inhale a little bit of their smoke, and some definitely take in more than others. The idea, however, is to savor the smoke in your mouth, not to draw it into your lungs.

What is coring, and what can I do to prevent it?

A cigar that burns faster in the center than on the sides is doing what's known as coring. It's usually caused by uneven construction inside the cigar—in particular, by an actual hole in the bunch created by the cigar roller. You can also cause it by uneven lighting. Make sure the entire foot of the cigar is burning when you begin puffing on it.

There's really not much you can do to prevent a cigar from coring once it's started. Sometimes the problem will correct itself as you smoke the cigar down. Smoking it slowly can help control the burn in the core.

You can hold your cigar in any of a number of ways. Shorter, thinner cigars, and especially cigarillos, can be held between the index and middle fingers as you would a cigarette. Due to their size, larger cigars such as Churchills, torpedoes, and robustos are often more comfortable between the index finger and the thumb, or between the thumb and the first three fingers. Let comfort be your guide.

How far down should I smoke my cigar?

The basic answer to this question is that you should smoke it until it doesn't taste good. Where this is will vary from cigar to cigar. Some will start to taste bitter or hot about halfway through, especially if you've smoked it too fast. Others, such as the Partagas 150 I just finished as I wrote this, will tempt you to burn your fingers (where is that old roach clip, anyway?).

Cigars are meant to be savored, which means smoking them slowly. How slowly is really up to you, as everyone has their own special rhythm or pace when it comes to smoking. As a guideline, a well-constructed, will-lit cigar should allow you to take about a puff or so a minute without the cigar going out. Smoking them too fast can make them burn too hot, which can produce a less-than-satisfactory smoke.

Cigars are meant to spend more time in your hand than in your mouth, but go ahead and hold your cigar in your mouth between puffs if you want to and you can do so comfortably. The head of the cigar will be wetter than if it spends more of its time in your hand or an ashtray, which doesn't look the greatest but in no way affects the way the cigar will smoke (in fact, some people feel it enhances the way the cigar smokes). This smoking style tends to make my hair smell more smoky and it fogs my contacts, two things you may want to keep in mind.

My cigar keeps falling out of my ashtray. What kind of ashtray should I use?

Standard-sized cigarette ashtrays really are too small to accommodate many cigars and should only be used for smaller cigars. Custom ashtrays specially designed for cigars, and in many price ranges, are available at most tobacconists. Some are teardrop-shaped and will cradle one cigar; others can handle communal smoking and have wide lips to balance the cigars on. Regardless of your preference in style, look for one that will hold your cigar horizontally when parked so that the cigar can continue to burn evenly. Also, it should have enough heft so that a heavy cigar won't tip it over when placed.

If, as you're savoring your cigar, it does go out on you, don't hesitate to relight it. Most cigars are made well and will burn consistently and evenly, even when smoked slowly. However, if yours doesn't, it doesn't mean it's a bad cigar. Some brands of cigars are packed tighter than others, and even those that aren't noted for this will go out on occasion, and they should go out if left sitting in an ashtray long enough. Interestingly, some cigars that go out and are relit taste even better the second time around. However, not all do. Let your taste buds be your guide.

How do I get rid of the aroma in my house, clothes, and hair?

Again, whether or not this is a problem varies from smoker to smoker. Personally, I like the aroma of cigar smoke on my clothing and in my smoking room (most of my clothing is stored in the same room, so I don't have much choice). Cigar smoke never smells as stale to me as cigarette smoke, but if it's a problem, especially for those around you . . .

Try limiting your smoking to one very well-ventilated room, preferably on an upper level (smoke rises, as you should well know). A small window fan, directed to the outside, can help dispel cigar smoke as it accumulates. An auxiliary air cleaner, ionizer, or filter in that room can also be helpful; just be sure to change the filters often as they do lose their effectiveness over time. Once you're done smoking, place your cigar stubs and ashes in a garbage bag and throw them away outside. Don't add them to family trash as they will continue to exude their aroma, and now they *will* smell pretty bad. Even I think stale cigar butts and ashes smell pretty awful.

There are also special sprays you can try to remove the smell of smoke from the air. The best of them actually neutralize the smell, rather than mask it. Your tobacconist may have one or more for you to choose from. Some of them can also be used on upholstery.

To remove the aroma from your clothing, try the following trick, which I read about in another book on cigars. Put your clothes on hangers and wrap them in a cleaner's bag. Shake a box or so of baking soda into the bottom of the bag, and let them hang for a day or so. The baking soda, which is a natural deodorizer, should neutralize the cigar smoke. I have tried this and it does work.

Washing your hair is about the only way to remove the smell of smoke, and a good thorough shampoo should take care of any remaining smoke aroma. Some hair products seem to grab hold of smoke smells more than others, but I'm not sure it's worth the time and expense to find the ones that don't.

The cigar I just smoked had little tiny white spots on its ash. What caused this?

Those white spots, called tooth, usually indicate the tiny pockets of oil that help give cigar wrappers their flavor. They're often seen in a Cameroon wrapper.

MINDING YOUR ASH

Sooner or later, you'll have to deal with the residue at the burning end of your cigar. If you're just smoking along, admiring your cigar and the smoke it produces, you've probably also been keeping an eye on your ash, watching it grow long, perhaps admiring its color. You might have an inch or so of ash by now. At this point, it may have developed a small crack running horizontally with the body of the cigar. If so, the ash is probably ready to be knocked off.

Why do some cigars produce a nice, tightly packed ash, but others tend to spew ash down the front of my shirt when I smoke them?

This is largely caused by the way the cigar was constructed. A well-constructed cigar will produce a firm ash that you remove by gently knocking it into an ashtray. Looser cigars will tend to drop some ash. By the way, the best way to remove ash that has fallen in this fashion is to gently flick it away from your clothing from the inside of the shirt, jacket, or whatever. Just give it a slight punch from the back, and the ash should fly away.

When it comes time to dispose of the ash, tap the side of the cigar against an ashtray or just touch the foot to the bottom of an ashtray. The ash should readily release, revealing the glowing core of the cigar. If it doesn't easily drop, wait a few minutes and try again as there may be leaf inside the cigar that is burning more slowly, hampering the deployment of the ash. Don't smack the cigar against the ashtray, as doing so may cause the wrapper to crack.

WHEN AND WHERE TO SMOKE

After dinner, either with or without spirits, is the classic time to savor a fine cigar. Personally, I can't think of a better way to draw a day to a close, either alone or with my husband, and I most often limit my enjoyment to this very special time. However, the many different types of cigars available today assure you of finding the perfect accompaniment to all occasions at any time of day.

For convenience sake, I tend to prefer smoking my cigars at home, where I have a specific room set aside for my smoking pleasure and I am surrounded by everything near and dear to me; however, more socially inclined cigar smokers will find a number of cigar-friendly restaurants, bars, and other establishments both across the United States and abroad. It's always advisable to call ahead and check the smoking policy at your intended destination; some establishments will vary the areas and hours that cigar smoking is allowed for seasonal and other reasons. Several cigar-related publications have good lists of cigar-friendly establishments; check chapter 8 for more information.

If, as you're enjoying your cigar in the smoking area at a cigar-friendly establishment, you are requested to extinguish your cigar by a non–cigar smoker, ask to speak to the management. They're the ones who established the smoking policy, and they should be the ones to enforce it.

What causes the color of the smoke?

Take a look at any ad for a Cuban cigar, and you'll notice the incredibly blue color of the smoke rising from the Habanos S.A. logo. Cuban cigars do have beautiful blue smoke, almost sapphire-colored in some. The smoke from other cigars will range from various shades of blue (nowhere near the deep blue of the Cuban cigars) to shades of gray. Again, it tends to indicate the type of tobacco used, not the quality of the cigar.

Many cigar-friendly establishments will have an assortment of cigars for you to select from, some better than others, and more often than not on the expensive side. You are also welcome to bring your own, which to many is the mark of a true cigar connoisseur.

CARRYING YOUR CIGARS

If you choose to travel with your cigars to the golf course or even just down to the corner bar for a drink, it's a good idea to protect them with something other than your shirt or jacket pocket or purse. Most beginning smokers fail to see the importance of this, but consider how you might feel when you crack the wrapper on your first premium cigar when you casually toss it into your purse or shirt pocket. Buy a cigar case before you get to that point. You'll be glad you did.

I want to take a few cigars to dinner with me, but don't want to just stick them in my coat pocket. What do you suggest?

Pocket cigar cases are the way to go. Not only do they protect your cigars, they also make a nice fashion statement. They come in a variety of sizes and are made from various materials, leather being the most available and popular. They're also a good choice for women wishing to carry their cigars in their purses.

Most tobacconists carry a selection of cigar cases in various sizes, styles, materials, and prices. They're worth the investment if you regularly smoke away from home. Choose a telescoping case if you smoke a variety of cigar styles, and consider buying a case that will house one more cigar than you think is necessary. Trust me.

I'm going on vacation next week and would like to take some cigars with me. What's the best way to pack them?

One of the best and cheapest ways to pack cigars in luggage is to fashion a travel humidor out of a small airtight plastic storage device. Make yourself a small traveling humidification device as well, or buy a cheap one.

Attractive travel humidors are also available from most tobacconists. They come in a range of sizes and prices. Make sure when you're buying one that it has enough capacity to keep you in cigars for the duration of your trip.

5

∞

Storing Your Private Collection

*Choice and expensive cigars . . . require
far more attention than they often receive.*

ALFRED H. DUNHILL, *THE GENTLE ART OF SMOKING*

If you're just beginning to smoke cigars, still experimenting with brands and styles, and buying just a few at a time and smoking them pretty quickly, storing them might not seem like much of an issue. It should be. If your purchases have been properly cared for by a tobacconist, a day or two removed from the controlled environment of their old home probably won't hurt them much. However, unless you're planning on smoking what you have on hand in the matter of a few days, you will run the risk of seriously affecting their quality, *and* diminishing your enjoyment of them, unless you are able to store them in an environment roughly equivalent to that of their former home.

I was just given some cigars that supposedly have been stored in a humidor for thirty years. Are they still smokable?

If they were stored properly, absolutely! I've heard stories of people who still have pre-Castro Cubans sitting in the dark recesses of their humidors.

Proper cigar storage is a subject of much discourse among cigar smokers. The options range from none at all (a bad idea, and best limited to inexpensive packaged cigars such as you would buy at a drug or grocery store) to custom-made, walk-in humidors that can store hundreds of cigars and cost many thousands of dollars. Fortunately, there's a storage option for everyone, no matter how small or large your budget or stash of stogies.

I just inherited a humidor from my grandfather that is lined with something that looks like milky glass. Aren't humidors supposed to be lined with cedar? Can I use this one?

The humidor you have inherited is lined with either porcelain, or, as you have aptly described, milk glass. Both substances were used in many older humidors, and since they're not very porous, they neither have an aroma of their own, nor will they absorb odors from other sources. Because of this, they won't enhance the flavor of the cigars you store in your humidor. Adding some cedar strips will. Absolutely, go ahead and use it, unless you have some reason to believe that it has construction problems that might affect its storage capabilities.

Again, this is an area where a good tobacconist can be very helpful. Most retailers have a supply of humidification products on hand, ranging from simple clay devices that you merely drop into a plastic bag to handsome humidors in at least several sizes, finishes, and price ranges.

ACHIEVING MAXIMUM SMOKABILITY

Cigars, because they are composed of an organic substance, are sensitive to their surroundings and will change over time. They're most comfortable in an environment with a relative humidity and temperature roughly equivalent to where they were manufactured. Notice, however, that I say *roughly*. There are some important differences, which I'll describe in more detail later.

What does it mean to age a cigar? Will this process improve my cigars?

Aging cigars is exactly what the name implies. It's a period of time during which the cigars are put to rest in a place where they'll be undisturbed and allowed to evolve and mature, much like what happens when they're aged during the manufacturing process.

Some cigar lovers, especially those in the United Kingdom, feel that aging cigars for a significant period of time—say, over five years—is essential to developing the true nature of a cigar. I've even read of some connoisseurs who are now enjoying cigars that are anywhere from twenty to forty years old (of course, they've been properly humidified the entire time). Obviously, they're a much more patient lot than most Americans, who have a hard time putting cigars away for several months, much less several years.

As far as whether or not aging will improve your cigars, unfortunately, only time will tell. Certainly, it takes some cigars longer to reach their prime than others. A case in point is the La Gloria Cubana that is manufactured in Miami, a cigar that is legendary for being somewhat green when it arrives at the tobacconist.

Because cigars change over time, storing them properly allows them to continue to age and mature to their fullest potential. This varies between cigars, and it's a known fact that certain tobaccos yield better results when aged than others. Some will hit a peak after a certain period of time and stay at that level; others may continue to improve or actually worsen over time. Again, maintaining a proper environment will enable them to become their very best, whatever it may be.

What is a green cigar?

When referring to cigars, green most often describes the way the cigar tastes, rather than its color (although there *are* green-colored cigars).

A green cigar is, basically, a young or fresh cigar. It is a cigar that hasn't undergone sufficient aging necessary for marrying its flavors or developing its character.

You'll know you're smoking a green cigar when it tastes of grass—the type found on lawns. Some cigars can be green and still taste pretty good. Others should be put into a humidor and aged.

BALANCING HUMIDITY AND TEMPERATURE

Cigars that are properly stored will have a healthy feel to them. If you press on them lightly, they'll spring back to their original shape. They'll have a weight that feels appropriate to their size, and they'll just generally look good. When you light them, they burn evenly and consistently, and they are a delight to smoke. This is what you're aiming for when you store your cigars, and it's achieved by balancing two factors in their environment: temperature and humidity.

Basically, when dealing with cigars, the goal is to create a constant environment of between 70 to 72 percent humidity, and between 68 to 70 degrees Fahrenheit. This balance, within a few degrees either way for both, isn't too critical, but beyond that, it is. At 68 percent humidity, cigars will slowly begin to dry out and lose the oils in their wrappers and fillers. At 74 percent humidity or higher, they can become mushy as their organic structure begins to break down. At 80 percent humidity or higher, you run the risk of growing mold, a definitely undesirable element in any cigar environment. Too low a temperature, while not necessarily damaging to cigars, will impede their maturing. Too high, and you may see another highly undesirable occupant in your storage device—Lacioderma, otherwise known as the evil cigar bug. More about them later.

Help! My favorite cigars look like they're turning gray.

What you're seeing (I hope!) is something called bloom, which happens when the oils in a cigar wrapper rise to the surface of the wrapper. In some humidors, you may notice cigars that look like they have little crystals on their surface. That's the first indication of bloom, and it can progress from there, making a cigar look dusty or whitish. This is a harmless condition, and in some cases, seeing bloom indicates a well-aged cigar. Just brush it off when you're ready to smoke your cigar.

If it's more than this, you do have a problem. Overhumidification of cigars (going over 85 percent) can cause mold, which you can easily recognize by comparing it to anything you've ever seen grow in your refrigerator.

Since mold spreads by spores, you absolutely have to get rid of any cigars sporting it immediately, as it will contaminate your other cigars, and, worse yet, spread to the wood in your humidor if you're using a wood humidor (this, however, tends to be more of a problem with those using plastic storage devices, and it usually happens when folks use plain water in their humidification devices).

After you've removed the moldy cigars, you also need to disinfect your humidor and, hopefully, save the other cigars from sprouting mold. Start by taking everything out of your humidor, and wiping down the entire interior with isopropyl alcohol. After doing this, let it air out (opened) for a few days. Next, you need to disinfect your humidification device. If it's homemade, throw it out and start over. If you're using a commercial device, you can try pouring boiling water through it, but be careful, as this can also melt the parts on plastic devices).

Now, on to your poor cigars. Wipe them off with a clean paper towel, moistened with distilled water. If you have cigars stored in cellophane, unwrap them and wipe them off as well. The cellophane will not protect them from the microscopic mold spores. When done, put them in a baggie or other storage device, away from your other cigars, and put them in the refrigerator. The cold will retard the growth of the mold.

Check them every couple of days or so for a week. If you don't see additional mold growth, take them out of the fridge and leave them at room temperature. Smoke them if you want. If you still don't see any mold after another week or so, you can probably put them back in your humidor.

Depending on where you live and the time of year, the proper environment can be somewhat easily achieved or nearly impossible to accomplish without the proper storage and humidification devices. Fortunately, most of us live or work in environments where the ambient temperature hovers around 70 degrees. Conveniently, this temperature is often found in closets, which are pretty good places to store cigars. So our primary concern is humidity.

Can I store a half-smoked cigar?

Definitely a better idea than leaving it in an ashtray till the next day. I keep a few extra ziplock bags from my cigar-shopping excursions in a cigar box near my smoking chair especially for this purpose. Just knock off the ash and pocket your cigar away (make sure it's out first, though). Keep your half-smoked stogies away from the others so there's no chance of your fresh cigars beginning to smell like your half-smoked ones. There's also a plastic device called the Cigar Savor that was made specifically for storing half-finished cigars. I've talked to several cigar smokers who have used this device with great success.

GETTING MOIST

The devices used to provide humidity for cigars run the gamut from commercial systems capable of maintaining hundreds of cigars to simple devices you can rig up yourself at home. Let your budget, your cigar storage needs, and your creativity be your guides as you figure out what will work the best for you.

For a long time, I rarely bought more than a few cigars at a time, and I was able to get by with a simple clay moisturizer. Costing less than $5, these simple devices usually resemble a piece of chalk encased in a metal slipcover. You slide the clay piece out and stick it into a cup of water for about fifteen minutes—long enough for the clay to change to a darker color, which signifies that it has soaked up as much water as it can hold. Remove it, wipe off the excess moisture, reinsert it into its holder, and you're ready to go. I usually put my clay device into a plastic bag with my cigars, which I would then put into an old Tabacalera cigar box left over from my father's smoking days. You can usually pick up an empty cigar box either free or for a dollar or two at your tobacconist. While it's not entirely necessary, the cedar lining lends a great aroma to your stash, and I know I always felt better having my cigars protected in a hard box as opposed to a soft plastic bag. You can also use a clay device in any other small storage device, and they work well as portable humidification devices when you're traveling. Be sure to check the clay every few days or so; when it begins to fade back to its original color, it needs to be rehydrated.

Another option, very similar to the clay stick humidifier, is the Humistat, which is a small, simple tube and sponge device available at many tobacconists. Also an inexpensive device, it's charged by filling the tube with water, which the sponge then soaks up. When done, reseal the top to keep the water inside the tube, and turn the bottom cap to cover or uncover as many air holes by the sponge as you think you might need to humidify your cigars. This, again, is a nifty device for humidifying cigars when you're traveling as it's small enough to fit into very limited spaces. Because of its size, however, it's not effective for humidifying large amounts of cigars.

Another relatively inexpensive commercial option is a product called the Humatic. It's available in several sizes: one will keep 50 cigars humidified, the other works on loads up to 125 cigars. All you have to do is tear open the top (the envelope contains a premoistened humidification device) and toss it into whatever storage device you're using. According to the manufacturer, the Humatic will maintain a constant relative humidity of 70 to 72 percent at 70 degrees Fahrenheit, and it will keep its charges humidified for a minimum of one year. These devices can't be easier to use. They're not as cheap as some other methods, but you can't beat the convenience.

I forgot to reseal the baggie that I got my cigars in, and now they feel hard and dry. Can I rehumidify them?

The short answer is yes, but it's not that easy to do. The best way is by slowly rehumidifying them in a proper humidor. If you don't have one, try taking them back to the tobacconist where you bought them and asking him if he's willing to let you stick your baggie in a deep corner of his humidor for a few days. It won't hurt to buy a few replacement cigars at the same time to smoke while your other cigars are (hopefully) recovering.

Lacking a proper humidor or a local friendly tobacconist, you can try rehumidifying them yourself. This procedure is largely based on trial and error and intuition, but briefly, place the open bag or box of cigars in a large plastic bag, partially but not completely closed so that you get some air flow. Put a glass of water or a moist sponge in the bag. Rotate the cigars every few days so that they all get evenly rehumidified.

Perhaps the best-known of the commercial devices is the Credo System. The Credo is a thick black or gold disk with ventilation holes on the top, revealing its internal humidifying reservoir, which contains propylene glycol. It comes in two sizes, depending on how many cigars you need to maintain: the Rondo, capable of handling 25 to 50 cigars, and the Precision 70, which is capable of handling 75 to 100 cigars. For larger storage requirements, multiple Credos can be used.

Prior to inserting it into whatever you're using for a storage device, you must activate the humidifying reservoir by adding distilled water until the unit is saturated but not soaked. There, it combines with the propylene glycol already residing in the reservoir to create a self-regulating humidification device; that is, it will maintain a constant 70 percent relative humidity if you can maintain the temperature at 70 degrees Fahrenheit. The propylene glycol allows this to happen because it releases moisture when the relative humidity is too low and absorbs moisture when the relative humidity is too high.

How often you refill a Credo with water will depend on a number of factors, including the capacity of your storage device, how many cigars you're storing, how often the device is opened, etc. If you're conditioning a new humidor, you may have to recharge the humidifying device more frequently until the cedar lining absorbs the appropriate amount of humidity.

The propylene glycol in Credo devices slowly evaporates over time. After a few months, you'll need to recharge the unit with Credo Juice, a fifty–fifty mix of water and propylene glycol available (under a variety of names) at most tobacconists.

BUILDING YOUR OWN HUMIDIFYING DEVICE

The elements used to construct a Credo are relatively inexpensive and easy to find, and you may be asking yourself, "Why don't I just make my own?" Well, you can. Use a small sponge, or, better yet, go to a florist or craft shop and buy a cube of Oasis, which is a green foam used in arranging flowers. There are two different types; you want to buy wet Oasis, which will do a better job of absorbing the water and propylene glycol you will fill it with. Next, head over to your local druggist and ask for a bottle of propylene glycol (it's used in formulating certain medications). If they don't have it, they might be willing to order it for you. A pint, which will keep you in good stead for a long time, will cost less than $10. Other places you might find propylene glycol include hobby shops and hardware stores.

Take your sponge or your Oasis block and soak it with the propylene glycol. Once it seems saturated, start adding distilled water until the sponge or Oasis won't accept it. Then place the sponge or Oasis in a ventilated container (a traveling soap box or an empty soft butter container with lots of holes punched in it work well). The container should be large enough to allow the sponge or Oasis to rattle around a bit. Then place it in your storage container.

You may need to experiment some with the size of your home-made Credo to determine the best humidifying effects for your cigars. One last thing to keep in mind: Regardless of what you end up using as a humidifying device, be sure to keep it away from direct contact with your cigars. It can ruin their wrappers.

WHY DISTILLED WATER?

Throughout the discussion of humidification, you may have noticed that I've recommended distilled water for filling the humidification device of your choice. Although it's always easiest to just open your water tap and use what's available, I strongly encourage you to buy a bottle of distilled water for your cigars (you can use it in your iron, too). The reason for this is that nondistilled water contains microbes that can adversely affect your cigars and cause mold, and ordinary tap water is treated with various chemicals. Although you might not catch the aroma of chlorine or other additives when you're washing your dishes or taking a shower, it can definitely permeate the cigars you have locked away in a closed environment.

The trace elements in tap water will also clog clay-type humidification devices, eventually robbing them of their effectiveness. Use distilled! Your cigars will thank you.

KEEPING COOL (RELATIVELY)

The second factor affecting cigar storage is temperature. Too low a temperature won't necessarily affect cigars adversely, but it will impede their maturation. Too high a temperature, however, can cause real problems.

The ideal temperature is similar to the ideal humidity—70 degrees Fahrenheit—which makes it pretty easy to remember. This temperature is cooler than what you'll generally find in the tropical climes where tobacco is grown and cigars are made, and there's a reason for it. Go much higher than 70 or 72 degrees, and you're likely to spur the development of Lacioderma, or the tobacco worm.

These little worms are largely controlled by tobacco growers, who routinely fumigate their storage and manufacturing facilities for them. However, even the Orkin man will tell you that the best fumigators in the business can't remove every little pest. One or two (or more) are bound to escape the fumes and will take refuge in the nearest tobacco leaves, where they will lay their eggs. Those eggs will stay dormant until something causes their arousal. That something is usually warmth, and especially warmth combined with humidity.

Most cigar smokers will go for years, perhaps even their lifetimes, without ever discovering a cigar worm, and, since they're incredibly tiny, you'll probably not see it even when it does decide to hatch. But you'll know for sure when you have them from the trail of destruction they leave behind, either in the form of a bore hole or a trail in the side of your favorite cigar. Sometimes, if you're exceptionally lucky (I jest), you'll see a teeny little beetle fly out of a cigar box as you open it (that's the worm, which has now metamorphosed into a bug), or you'll find its dead body at the bottom of the box.

Help! My favorite cigar has a little hole in its side that I just know was caused by the evil cigar bug Lacioderma. You promised you'd tell me what to do!

Help is on the way! Remove the wounded cigar and all its buddies from your storage device, and inspect them to see if any others are sporting the same hole. If they are, you may want to throw them out. It won't hurt you, however, if you decide to take your chances and smoke one. The worst thing that will happen is that the hole bored by the little devil will affect the way the cigar smokes.

While your cigars are out of their storage device, take the opportunity to clean it thoroughly. If you have cigars that appear to be healthy, put them in a plastic bag and freeze them for two or three days. This will kill the rest of the bugs. After their tour in the freezer, slowly return them to room temperature by moving them into the refrigerator until they thaw. You'll be able to tell when they're defrosted by squeezing them slightly—there should be some give to them. Don't hurry this process, as doing so can result in cracked wrappers.

If you should find a dead body, don't assume that the cigars that show no evidence of infestation are safe. They aren't. See the sidebar on page 81 for advice on how to get rid of the rest of the pests.

Fortunately, most of us live in environments where the ambient indoor temperature hovers at 70 degrees, and at that temperature you're almost sure to never meet up with Mr. Lacioderma. If yours is hotter, keep your cigars in a dark closet, preferably on the main floor of your residence, since heat rises. Basements can also be good spots—mine stays at 70 degrees for the entire spring and summer, and since my office is down there, I use a small space heater during fall and winter to keep the temperature in roughly the same range.

Ambient temperatures in homes and offices change as the seasons change, and you may have to move your cigar storage in light of that. Not long ago, a good friend called me with some concerns over the expensive humidor he had purchased several months ago. It had started out keeping the cigars perfectly, but now his stash seemed to be drying out, regardless of how often he refilled his humidification device.

He was keeping his humidor on a desk near a window in his east-facing home office, which was fine during the summer when the trees outside the windows of his office shaded the interior and kept the temperature low. But in fall, the leaves were off the trees, and his poor humidor was sitting in direct sun for several hours every day. Even the best humidor has problems keeping its humidity levels high when it's baking in 90-degree heat. We discussed two options: installing drapes or blinds to cut the fall and winter sun, or moving the humidor to a cooler spot for the season. Not desiring to obstruct his view of the mountains, he chose to move the humidor.

If you're the kind of smoker who travels with his or her cigars, also keep in mind that leaving them in a closed car can ruin them. Just like other items of a perishable nature—animals, small children, records, photography equipment, videotapes, chocolates, etc.—your cigars will perish if exposed to the high temperatures so readily and quickly achieved in a closed car. Take your cigars with you if you intend to leave your car for more than a minute or so. Or, put them in your trunk and park in the shade. If you frequently take your cigars on your travels, consider buying an insulated storage case. Cigar Classics makes one specially for cigars built into a Zero Halliburton case—the type of case used by photographers and others working with delicate equipment. It holds roughly thirty cigars and has a digital hygro-thermometer and a humidifying device built into its lid.

ABOUT REFRIGERATION

I don't think there's a cigar smoker out there who hasn't stored his or her cigars in a refrigerator at least once. Some people even think it's a good idea to do so. It isn't! Do not, I repeat, *do not* store your cigars in a refrigerator, even overnight. It's too cold in there for them, and the relative humidity in most refrigerators, due to the constant air circulation necessary for the frost-free feature found in most of today's refrigerators, is way below where it needs to be for a cigar to be happy. If you've ever left a piece of fruit or a vegetable unwrapped in your fridge (and who among us hasn't?), only to find it shriveled and puckered on the top, know that the same thing will happen to anything else of a vegetal nature, which cigars certainly are! Even if the cigars you've purchased are cellophaned, they will dry out. I found this out, sadly enough, when, soon after I started smoking cigars, I stuck a handful I had purchased at the last minute into a friend's refrigerator for safekeeping before a dinner party. The cigars got pushed to the back of the refrigerator and I forgot I'd bought them until several days later when I pulled the receipt out of my purse. I was able to rehumidify them, but why go through the hassle when you can easily prevent it from happening at all! Even rehumidified, they smoked a little funny, and they were slightly redolent of the roasted chili peppers my friend had stored in her freezer. You're better off sticking them in the dark recesses of a main-floor closet with a little wad of moistened tissue until you can get them properly stored.

KEEPING CONSTANT

The final variable to consider when storing cigars is maintaining a consistent environment. This is important because wide variations in humidity and temperature can cause cigar wrappers to crack, which, depending on the severity of the crack and the type of wrapper, can severely diminish the smokability of the cigar. Over-humidification causes this more than anything else. Be sure to check your cigars regularly as well as the humidity level of your storage device to make sure your humidifying device is doing its job. (More on how to do this later.)

I lit my cigar a few minutes ago, and now that I have it burning, I'm noticing a number of small cracks appearing in the wrapper. They seem to be getting worse as I smoke.

This is caused by uneven humidification conditions. It also can be exacerbated by the way you handle your cigar, especially if you're smoking one with a delicate wrapper that is easily cracked. Ex-cigarette smokers, in particular, are often at fault for causing these small cracks as they tend to twirl the cigar in their hands as they smoke them. A good rule of thumb is to always handle your cigar gently, and don't keep spinning it around to look at it. Small cracks can often be repaired in some wrappers (especially delicate Connecticut shade) by moistening them.

CHOOSING A STORAGE DEVICE

Now that you know the basics of cigar storage, it's time to decide on the device in which you will store your charges. There's a broad range of options here; again, let your storage needs, your budget, and your inventiveness be your guide in selecting the right ones for you.

Tobacconists routinely stock a number of storage devices. The cheapest is going to be an empty cigar box, which most retailers will part with for free or for a dollar or so. I know occasional cigar smokers who have used old boxes for years, properly outfitted with plastic baggies and inexpensive humidifying devices. Even the tightest cigar box isn't airtight; make sure you give the cigars adequate protection against drying out.

The next option is an inexpensive humidor. There's a relatively inexpensive plastic variety available with a rechargeable humidification device built into the lid. These can work just fine, but be sure to check the sides where the edges join to make sure they're as tight as possible. Plastic or Lucite boxes are notorious for air leakage; if the sides and seams don't match, too much humidity will escape, defeating the reason you bought your humidor.

Cigar jars are another inexpensive option favored by some cigar smokers. They're pretty much what the name implies: a tall jar, often resembling an old-fashioned apothecary or spaghetti jar, with a sponge built into the lid. There's even a style available that allows you to customize the flavor of your cigars by adding your favorite cognac, bourbon, or whatever to the humidifying device. Plan to spend around $55 or so for the basic jar; the aromatic style costs more due to the special devices necessary for transferring the alcoholic influences to your cigars. When using a cigar jar, keep an eye on the heads and feet of your cigars; vertical storage can damage them. Also, don't load them too full or you may have to remove all the cigars in order to retrieve the small ones that will drop to the bottom of the jar.

From here, the sky is truly the limit. Handsome humidors constructed from the finest hardwoods just beg to be filled with the best cigars from your collection. Ranging in size from travel and desktop models that store a handful of cigars to elaborate cabinet styles that can take up residence in the most lavishly appointed office or home, these humidors range significantly in price based on their size, construction, materials, and finish. Some of the finest are made by Elie Bleu, Daniel Marshall, Michel Perrenoud, J. C. Pendergast, and others, and they come at a price, believe me!

Will adding some of my favorite spices and flavorings to my humidor, such as nutmeg and vanilla, enhance the natural flavors of my cigars?

Each cigar is different, and you may end up with some overly heady flavorings that will overpower your cigars. If you want to try adding some aromas to your cigars, there's a product available called Cigaroma that allows you to infuse your cigars with spirits. Check with your local tobacconist or at the company's Web site <http://www.cigaroma.com>, which also gives a list of retailers.

Whether you're planning to spend a couple of hundred or several thousand dollars on a humidor, there are several things you should look for when shopping for one. If it doesn't have these elements, put it aside and look at another one. Don't allow yourself to be swayed by the elegance of the humidor's style, its appointments, or its finish.

First, inspect the outside of the box. All joints and seams should be even and closely fitted together. There should be no apparent gaps between the body of the box and the lid, as they will be a conduit for moisture evaporation. Then, lift the lid and let it drop lightly. It should feel heavy, and when dropped, should meet the body of the humidor with a slight *whoosh,* signifying the rush of escaping air as the humidor seals itself.

Open the humidor. Inside, you should again see perfectly squared corners and fitted seams. If it's cedar-lined, as most humidors are these days, the cedar should feel silky and smooth to the touch. It should also be unfinished. Make sure there's an inner lip that sticks out from around the body of the humidor into the lid, which will help seal the box and prevent moisture loss.

Major factors to consider when selecting a humidor include the size and the amount of cigars you wish to store. Make sure the humidor you choose can house the cigars you enjoy smoking; a small humidor rated for storing two dozen cigars might not be able to accommodate the corona gordos you've come to like. Also, humidors are meant to be kept no more than three-quarters full in order to allow the cigars to breathe. If you can afford it, buy a humidor in the next size up from the one you began contemplating. Most people find that their cigar collection immediately swells once their new humidor arrives home—mine certainly did!

If your heart is set on buying a humidor, I encourage you to decide on a price range that you're willing to spend and buy the best humidor available within that range. Let quality, rather than capacity, govern your choice. Although it may be tempting to buy that large humidor that seems to be such a good deal at $250, you may end up with a cheaply made product that will do your cigars more harm than good over the long run.

Many fine humidors are available through catalogs and mail order, but you're probably better off buying your first one at a local shop, where you can rely on the guidance and advice of your tobacconist. Buying any product sight unseen asks for a certain leap of faith, no matter the price, and there's really nothing that replaces old-fashioned, hands-on screening when you're shopping for quality merchandise. Also, if you have any problems with your humidor, it's sometimes easier to rectify them through a local source, especially if you buy it from a tobacconist with whom you've established a good relationship, rather than with a nameless, faceless voice across long-distance wires.

I can't think of a cigar smoker, whether newcomer or seasoned pro, whose heart doesn't quicken just slightly at the sight of a beautifully constructed wood humidor, and a fine humidor is undeniably an excellent accompaniment—perhaps even a necessity—to a cigar lover's world, since a well-built and well-maintained humidor should virtually eliminate cigar storage problems. As a newcomer, however, your money is probably better spent on the objects of your desire than on the housing that will go around them.

Fortunately, with a little enterprise and a few inexpensive devices, you can create a humidor that can accommodate your growing collection of cigars quite nicely. Just go to your local supermarket, hardware, or discount store and purchase a plastic storage container with a seal-tight lid (if you don't already own one). Line the bottom with cedar strips, which your kindly tobacconist will most likely have an abundance of, and load it with your cigars and your humidifying device. If you have lots of cigars to store, or cigars of more than one type of tobacco that you don't want to marry, you may want to consider buying a few plastic silverware or makeup storage trays to nestle your cigars into. Using these trays can also make it easier to rotate your cigars if you're putting them down to age for a long period of time.

Plastic storage devices, while not the most aesthetically pleasing, provide a great way to store cigars, especially if you're getting to the point where you're finding brands and styles of cigars that you'd like to buy by the box, or you've come across some cigars that you feel might benefit by some long-term aging. If you're going to store your cigars in plastic, make sure you do add some cedar, which will enhance the flavor of the cigars you're storing. Also, their airtightness may cause some mustiness in your cigars if you leave it unopened for too long a time. Open the container every few days and let your cigars get a whiff of fresh air.

LEAVING CELLOPHANE ON OR TAKING IT OFF

Ask a number of cigar smokers this question, and you'll get a variety of answers. Some feel cigars won't age correctly in cellophane wrappers, others worry about the blending of characteristics that takes place when unwrapped cigars of more than one type are stored together.

The cellophane I just removed from my cigar feels oily. Is my cigar okay?

Absolutely! The oil you're seeing and feeling is a natural by-product of the aging of the wrapper. Some wrappers have more oil than others.

Part of the reason for storing cigars in humidors is allowing them to age. Just like wine, aging cigars involves chemical processes and changes. In the case of cigars, oxidation, other chemical changes, and the blending of essential oils are all involved. If you're aging a number of similar cigars, removing the cellophane wrappers surrounding them will allow the cigars to share their traits with one another. This process is called *marrying,* which will result in more consistency from one cigar to another. It doesn't, however, make any one cigar significantly better or worse.

Many people keep a variety of cigars in storage. If you're one of them, you're better off leaving the wrappers on. Because the ends of the wrappers are never sealed—they're just folded over—your cigars will still benefit from their humidified climate. Also leave the wrappers on if you keep an assortment available in a smaller box or humidor for daily use. Since these storage devices are opened more frequently than those used for long-term storage, you want to give your cigars as much protection as you can from the evaporation that will take place every time you open the humidor or box. Another good reason to leave the cellophane on your cigars is if you should have a change of heart about those cigars for any reason, or if you are unsatisfied with them and wish to return them.

A related question concerns leaving cigars in their boxes or removing them when putting them into storage. Again, the same principles apply. Cigars that are packed in a sealed, plastic-wrapped box, such as they are when they're shipped, will stay in roughly the same condition for quite a long time if stored correctly. However, they won't age or mature if kept sealed. If the box has been opened, and if you have enough space in your storage device to store that box, by all means do so. If not, take the cigars out and store them that way.

I would like to ship some cigars to my girlfriend as a surprise gift. What's the best way to do this?

If you're shipping just a few cigars, make sure they're packed in a very solid container in such a way that they won't move around much, and consider putting that container into another box with extra packing material to make sure they don't get crushed. Make sure the cigars are sealed in a plastic bag that you've squeezed all the air out of.

Regardless of whether you're shipping a few cigars or an entire box, send them the fastest way possible. Ground transportation means those cigars will be sitting in hot trucks and trains, and they're more likely to get dried out. Send them either second-day or next-day air for the best results. If you choose a carrier such as Federal Express or UPS, you can track their arrival as well, which is also desirable for more expensive shipments.

MEASURING

Finally, it's a good idea to measure the humidity in your cigar storage device. You do this by using an hygrometer, which is a mechanical or electronic device used for measuring relative humidity. Many commercially built humidors come with a hygrometer built into their lid along with their humidification device. They can range from simple dials to elaborate digital readouts that will also tell you the temperature inside the box.

Most tobacconists sell several different hygrometers. The most common are small dial-type analog hygrometers, which usually come in a chrome or brass housing. If possible, buy one that you can adjust either by turning its housing or by tinkering with it through an opening on its back. Many hygrometers will need adjusting, as the jostling they undergo when shipped will knock their calibration off somewhat. There are scientific ways to determine their accuracy (check chapter 8 for the Internet location that has detailed instructions), but the easiest way is to wrap the hygrometer in a wet towel for about an hour. When you remove the towel, the hygrometer should read 100 percent. Adjust accordingly if it's higher or lower.

6

Accompaniments

Until you've had a good cigar and a shot of whiskey,
you're missin' out on the second and third best things in life.

Tom Ligon as young Horton Fenty
in *Paint Your Wagon*

What goes well with a cigar? Maybe the better question is, what doesn't? Marrying cigars to beverages and foods is another delightful part of the cigar smoking experience, and you don't have to be a connoisseur of any of them to find the combinations that work best for you. Just combine a little experimentation with the many different types of cigars, foods, and beverages available, and you're sure to come up with your own favorite—and memorable—pairings.

There is a long tradition behind combining cigars with food and drink, which is now being echoed by the cigar dinners and smokers' nights that are becoming increasingly popular across the country. In Victorian times, when multicourse dinners were the norm, cigars were a major component of a successful evening, and, in fact, were often kept lit during the various courses as they were served and enjoyed. After dinner, the men repaired to their smoking rooms for their after-dinner cigars and ports.

Although it's somewhat traditional to limit cigar smoking to after dinner, there's no reason why you have to, with the many different styles and sizes of cigars available today. By all means, try smoking a cigar after a leisurely lunch out, while enjoying before-dinner cock-tails with your friends, or between courses at a long dinner (as long as you're in areas where cigar smoking is permitted). Although I'm in the category of smokers who usually limit enjoyment of cigars to after dinner, I often carry several miniature Macanudos with me when I go to business lunches, and I find myself sharing them with one or more of my luncheon guests more frequently these days as the interest in cigars continues to grow. (I should mention that many miniature cigars or cigarillos, especially the milder, less aromatic ones, will often escape the notice of other patrons if you're at an establishment that allows cigarette smoking but forbids cigars. It's worth a shot, but be prepared to put out your little cigar if someone does complain.)

There are really very few hard and fast rules when it comes to combining cigars with food and beverage. But . . . there are a few. I've listed some personal favorites as general suggestions for these pairings in this chapter. For more information on specific cigars that work in each category, turn to the next chapter.

COMPLEMENTS WORK

In general, you should choose your cigar to complement the type and style of food and beverage being served. Basically, the fuller and spicier the food, the fuller-bodied and spicier the cigars should be. The same principle applies to pairing cigars with alcohol, whether it's wine or spirits. You want to make sure your cigar will stand up to the level of flavor and spice in the meal; if it doesn't, your enjoy-ment of the cigar will be severely diminished as your poor taste buds will have a devil of a time tasting that cigar at all!

Your cigar choice should also complement the time of day at which you'll be smoking. At the beginning of each day, our palates start out at a distinctively fresher level than when they finish the day. This is a major reason why cigars taste different at different times of the day. If you choose to indulge in a cigar at any other time of the day than after dinner, make sure to take fullest advantage of the cigar you choose to smoke by selecting lighter, milder cigars for during-the-day smoking, especially if you're smoking in the morning or after a light lunch. Reserve your heavier, fuller-bodied cigars for dinnertime and after, when your palate has adjusted to the point where it will fully enjoy these cigars.

Meat

The menus at smokers' nights and dinners tend to run toward meat, with well-aged steaks, chops, and prime beef as the hallmarks of many of these menus. They are the classic accompaniments to what I used to call gentlemen's cigars: full, rich, and aromatic. This is the time to smoke the finest cigar you have, possibly Honduran, and maybe with a maduro wrapper. Consider a Hoyo de Monterrey Excalibur No. 1, or a Felipe Gregorio Glorioso (a double corona) or a Punch Grand Cru.

Seafood

Pairing cigars with seafood can be a bit more difficult, due to the delicate nature of most types of fish. Again, the way the fish is prepared has a great deal to do with the cigar you choose to accompany it. Spicier fish dishes such as paella—a wonderfully aromatic combination of rice, fish, shellfish, chicken, vegetables, and sausage—and bouillabaisse—a fish stew that features many different types of fish—certainly can stand up to the same full-bodied, rich cigars you would pair with meat. Shellfish, especially lobster, can be an excellent complement to creamier, smoother cigars, especially those from the Dominican Republic. Personal favorites here include Butera Royal Vintage in any size I can get my hands on, or any size from Astral as well.

Game

If you're lucky enough to have a game meal in your future, consider pairing it with a cigar with a little roughness to it; a classic game meal cigar, in my opinion, is the Henry Clay, which sports a dark, Connecticut broadleaf maduro wrapper. Or try a cigar from Nicaragua, especially one with a maduro wrapper. The slightly sweet taste to many of these cigars can make an interesting pairing with very savory game.

Pasta

If pasta is the main focus of your meal, let its sauce determine your cigar choice—again, a rich, full red sauce should go well with either Dominican or Honduran cigars. Several I like particularly well with pasta are the Avo XO or Paul Gamirian, which has a certain smooth spiciness to it.

There are some cuisines that just don't seem to pair up well with cigars. Try as I might, I can't think of a cigar I'd like to smoke after a sushi dinner; it seems almost sacrilegious to layer even the mildest smoke over the subtle fragrances and tastes of these Japanese morsels. Chinese food is another tough match, no matter what style it is, but there are cigars manufactured in China, so maybe I just haven't found the right combination yet.

CIGARS AND WINE

Wine and cigars is one of the world's most classic combinations, probably owing to the similarities between them. Both are composed of a blend of ingredients. Both are fermented and aged, and both have a point at which they will reach their peak.

The different pairings possible between your favorite grape and your favorite cigar are staggering. Just days prior to writing this section, I was on-line in a chat room on cigars when this topic came up. The overall consensus among the chat participants was that there were few wines that didn't combine well with cigars, except perhaps for the very cheapest boxed wines and Mogen David. Then someone came up with suggestions for them as well!

As is true with food and cigars, pair your fuller-bodied wines with cigars of the same characteristics. If you're a fan of lighter, fruitier whites or reds, choose cigars on the lighter side, such as Pleiades or Macanudos. As you work your way up the scale to fuller-bodied reds, such as Zinfandels and Cabernet Sauvignons, Honduran or

Nicaraguan cigars should be your choice. Personal favorites here include Puros Indios, The Griffins, Hoyo de Nicaragua, or anything from the Don Tomas Special Edition line.

PORT: THE CLASSIC CHOICE

Dating back to Victorian times, port has been one of the most famous accompaniments to an after-dinner cigar. If you've never tried it, you owe it to yourself to pay homage to this old tradition.

Port is a fortified wine, meaning that something is added to it to render it in its final state. In this case, brandy is added to the already fermented wine to increase its alcohol level and give it its characteristic sweetness. Because it's aged in wood, port can often take on the characteristics of its aging environment; it's not uncommon to hear someone describe a port as having a "cigar box" taste or aroma.

There are a number of different kinds of port available, ranging from reasonably priced to outrageous. Vintage port, which can take years to reach its market due to the aging process it undergoes, is often the most expensive and the most wonderful; nonvintage port is much less expensive and well worth trying. If you're unfamiliar with port, ask the staff at your local liquor or wine store for some recommendations. Some of the better-known port producers are Graham, Taylor, Cockburn, Sandeman, and Fonseca.

Pair them with fuller-bodied cigars, possibly with maduro wrappers, from Honduras or Nicaragua. I like anything from the Thomas Hinds Nicaraguan Selection or La Finca. Both are Nicaraguan puros. Another interesting choice here is the Fonseca Pyramid (yes, the same name as the port), a Dominican cigar with a rich, full flavor that marries well to lighter ports.

BRANDY AND COGNAC

These intense distilled spirits are also classic combinations with cigars. Combine a snifter of your favorite brand, either warmed or at room temperature, with a cup of coffee and a robust cigar for an extraordinary nightcap.

Depending on the strength of the brandy or cognac, cigar pairings here range from Dominicans to Hondurans. One cigar especially to try here is the El Sublimado, which is flavored with fifty-year-old Noces d'Or cognac.

THE SPIRIT OF SCOTCH

Whether your taste is for a blended Scotch such as Chivas Regal or Johnnie Walker, or you prefer the distinctive character of single-malt Scotch from any of the various regions of Scotland, there's probably no better combination than Scotch and a good cigar. This is a spirits/cigar combination that works well either before or after dinner; lighter blended Scotches, especially if mixed with water or soda, pair up well with Dominican cigars such as the Daniel Marshall, Avo, or Fonseca. Try them as well with a smoky or peaty single-malt Scotch, either neat or with a splash of water or on the rocks. Another wonderful pairing here is your favorite single malt with the El Incomparable, which is flavored with single-malt Scotch.

AMERICA'S OWN: BOURBON

Bourbon is beyond a doubt one of the best accompaniments to a late-night cigar. If you're familiar with such classics as Jim Beam, Ancient Age, and Wild Turkey, give your taste buds a treat and try one of the newer small batch bourbons, such as Knob Creek, Booker's 107, or Maker's Mark. I guarantee you'll be hooked! With these bourbons, it seems almost sacrilegious to smoke anything other than a Henry Clay, but any full-bodied cigar goes well here. One of my favorites is the Hoyo de Monterrey Excalibur No. 1 maduro if I have time to smoke it.

OTHER LIBATIONS

Fine cigars were traditionally enjoyed after dinner, and martinis were not a traditional accompaniment to them. However, this most famous of bar drinks, somewhat neglected during recent years, is making a much-heralded comeback across the country. There's probably not another drink with the elegance of a martini; if you're enjoying a before-dinner cigar, you should certainly consider pairing it with your favorite martini blend.

Rum, especially the darker, more aged varieties, is also receiving a second visit by many cigar smokers. Depending on the country of origin, rum can run the gamut from light to heavy and dark. Mild to medium Dominican, Honduran, or Nicaraguan cigars work well with rum.

Beer has come a long way from being a cheap brew to pair with a cheap cigar after mowing the lawn on a hot summer day. Today's microbrews are probably the hottest new combinations with cigars. Following your nose is often a good way to determine what cigar to select as many beers, especially the newer microbrews, are quite aromatic. Again, the deeper, fuller-bodied brews such as ales need cigars that can stand up to them; lighter, pilsner styles go nicely with lighter cigars such as the Temple Hall or Macanudo.

ON THE NONALCOHOLIC SIDE

I think most long-time cigar smokers will agree that just about any beverage goes well with a cigar. This is definitely an area where your smoking preferences and your taste buds need to be your guide. Don't be afraid to experiment. For a long time, I thought only cold or room-temperature beverages went well with cigars, but I changed my mind when, not too long ago on a cold snowy night, I had my first cup of hot chocolate with a Hoyo de Monterrey Excalibur No. 1, my favorite evening cigar when I can set aside the amount of time necessary to fully enjoy one. For a special treat, I add a shot of Scotch to my evening chocolate—a holdover from my camping days. It may sound crazy, but don't knock it until you try it.

Some teas are also wonderful accompaniments to cigars. In fact, iced tea is the traditional palate cleanser used by cigar tasters in Cuba. If you're tasting a number of cigars, use it or plain water to cleanse your palate. Try Lapsang Souchong, with its delightfully smoky taste, or any one of the fuller-bodied teas marketed as after-dinner teas if you drink your tea hot. Cha, the spiced Indian tea usually served with milk or cream, is also a wonderful accompaniment to a cigar. For iced tea, Lipton's, brewed a little strong, stands up well to even the strongest cigar.

I find most herbal teas too light and delicate to be sipped with a cigar. These teas are overwhelmed by even the mildest of them. On the other end of the spectrum, coffee seems to go to war with my taste buds when I pair it with my favorite cigars. However, I'm not much of a coffee lover, so I probably haven't tried enough different blends to find the ideal combination. If you do love coffee, by all means go ahead and give this combination a try.

Many people feel that sweetened beverages detract from the taste of the cigar. That could be true, and artificially sweetened beverages could perhaps lend an unwanted aftertaste to a good cigar, but then again, there are legions of people who enjoy pop, either sugar-fortified or diet, with their cigars. Truly, this is a case of individual palate. I've even been known to enjoy an Orange Crush on occasion with my favorite cigar. I'm not sure I'd try this with a grape-flavored beverage, but if that's what you like, by all means, give it a shot. A friend of mine plans his midday break around a Carlin corona and a Diet Coke. One of my girlfriends really enjoys 7Up with her Macanudos. It's truly a matter of choice.

WHAT ABOUT CHOCOLATE?

Chocolate and cigars is one of my most favorite after-dinner combinations, most likely due to my early predilection for maduro-wrapped cigars, which can often have a chocolately taste to them. Since I've almost never met a piece of chocolate I didn't like and I've also almost never had a cigar I didn't like, they are, at least for me, an easy and ready companion to a good after-dinner or dessert cigar. One absolutely perfect truffle, cream-or liquor-filled, is a beautiful companion to fuller-bodied cigars such as the Felipe Gregorio or the El Incomparable, or to cigars with a somewhat chocolately finish such as the Carlin corona. On the more pedestrian side, a handful of M&Ms, or a Hershey's bar or Kiss aren't to be overlooked, either. For an absolutely wonderful celebration, try a glass of good (or even not so good) champagne, a premium truffle or two from your favorite manufacturer, and your special long-smoking cigar. Oooh, what decadence. And the pleasure's all yours!

ABOUT SMOKERS' NIGHTS AND DINNERS

If you live in a city where local restaurants either occasionally or routinely sponsor such events, by all means consider attending one, either by yourself or with a companion. They're generally not terribly cheap, but when you consider all you get—usually a full dinner, plus complementing wines or other beverages and three or four cigars—they're not that expensive, either. Not only are they a great way to experience different wine/food/cigar combos, often selected by experts and maybe featuring cigars that are either new to your market or new to you, they're also a great way to meet and network with other cigar enthusiasts in your area. Ask your local tobacconist for a list of smokers' nights and dinners in your area—he or she may even sponsor them occasionally—or check the back pages of *Cigar Aficionado* magazine, which routinely lists establishments sponsoring such events.

7

Journeying
through Cigars

*It is each individual's perception of a particular cigar
that determines whether or not it is worthy of being smoked.*

RICHARD CARLTON HACKER, *THE ULTIMATE CIGAR BOOK*

One of the best parts about writing this book, at least so I thought in the beginning, would be conducting the research necessary for composing this section. Talk about your easy assignments! Getting paid for doing something I loved—what a concept!

Well, of course it didn't turn out to be as easy as I thought. As much as I enjoy cigars, the term *busman's holiday* took on new meaning for me as I smoked brand after brand, day after day and night after night, revisiting cigars I hadn't smoked for a long time, experiencing many new brands, or at least ones new to me, and rejudging my favorites for possible inclusion in this section. What was for so long a pleasurable pastime became a little too much like a job, albeit one that many would covet.

The other factor that quickly became evident is that, like most cigar smokers, I have my prejudices, and I tend to favor a handful of brands. I also tend to favor certain shapes and styles. So, because people's tastes vary so greatly, and there are so many factors that should be considered when selecting a cigar, I decided to ask for input from some of my cigar-smoking friends as well. These cigar enthusiasts run the gamut from a seasoned cigar veteran of over twenty years, to whom price is little if any object, to several recent college graduates who are always looking for the best cigar they can afford on their very limited incomes. Both men and women participated. Although we all have our own opinions, the nice thing about using a collection of opinions for this section was that we found a great deal of consensus among us when it came to deciding what we should and shouldn't include.

A good friend just gave me a box of cigars that I know I don't like. He, however, is thrilled over having bought me such a great gift and expects to see me light one up at our weekly poker sessions. How can I get around it?

You can try one of several approaches. The easiest is to tell your friend that you felt the box needed a little aging, and that it's resting in your humidor. Or, you can tell him the cigars were way too nice to smoke at a lowly poker game, and you're saving them for more special occasions.

These are exciting times for the cigar industry and for cigar enthusiasts alike. Although it can't be denied that prices are going up and selection can be somewhat limited for the most popular brands, this doesn't mean that the world of cigar smoking is going to pot as some would argue. The good news is that there are many, many wonderful cigars out there to be tried, and more being introduced by the day. Although we all enjoyed some cigars more than others, I can honestly say that there was only one cigar (which will go unnamed, although it came highly recommended) that most of us felt was truly bad.

What follows is a listing of the cigars we all liked for a variety of reasons and felt were worth recommending. Although I definitely liked some of these cigars better than others, I feel any of the cigars listed here are worthy of smoking; however, you might disagree on one, several, or more. You might feel I've not included some that I should have, or that I've included some that you think are absolutely unsmokable.

I tried to limit our choices to cigars that were available at our local tobacconists and priced within a reasonable budget. For this reason, you won't find opinions on some cigars that have received a great deal of press, such as the Fuente Fuente Opus X and the Diamond Crown, both of which were either unavailable locally or priced so ridiculously that we didn't feel justified in buying them. Some of the cigars you'll read about were readily available; others we snapped up when we were advised that a shipment had just arrived.

A word of advice related to availability: If you see a box of your favorite cigars at your local tobacconist and you're thinking about buying it, do so if you can afford it and if you have or can construct the appropriate storage facilities for your purchase. With supply and demand being what they are in today's cigar industry, you might wait months before you see your favorites again, especially if they're a premium brand in high demand. If you can't afford the entire box, buy what you can or see if you can split the purchase with a friend. I guarantee you won't regret it.

While I believe that following the advice of a good tobacconist is one of the best ways to select a cigar, the simple fact is that you, and you alone, will be the best judge of what you do and don't like in a cigar. And the only way to reach those conclusions is to smoke them for yourself. Many long-time cigar enthusiasts believe that the only way to truly judge a cigar is to smoke an entire box of them. Although there's some merit to this approach, adhering to it today would cost a lot more and take a great deal more time than the average cigar smoker has. I can tell you that I've smoked that many of just a handful of my favorites. To me, one of the greatest delights about smoking cigars is trying the variety of different brands available on today's market, as there's always something new to try, and my favorite cigar might end up being the next one I smoke. However, you should smoke more than one cigar of a certain brand before forming your opinion on the entire brand or before you begin extolling its virtues to others.

I would like to present my cousin with a box of cigars for his wedding, but I'm not sure what he likes to smoke and we don't live anywhere close. Should I go ahead and guess, or forget the whole idea?

What a nice cousin you are! Part of the answer on this one is determined by whether the cigars are for him personally or for the wedding party.

If they're for the wedding party, let your budget be your guide. If you can afford a pricey, premium cigar, by all means buy a box. If not, ask your local tobacconist for a recommendation in whatever price range you feel comfortable. Chances are, by the time the wedding party gets around to lighting them, they won't have a clue as to what they're smoking anyway!

If they're for your cousin's own use, there are certain cigars that are sure bets regardless of smoking preference. Ask your tobacconist for some recommendations. You can also consider giving a gift certificate to a local tobacconist so he can pick out exactly what he wants.

Perhaps the best way to approach what follows is to consider it a road map of sorts. By no means is it intended to be a comprehensive guide. If you get to the point where you want to purchase such an item, check several that are listed in the Resources section. They're usually published annually and they include the most up-to-date information on what's available.

To make things easy, it's arranged in alphabetical order by cigar brand. You'll find general information about each brand first (when the brand is produced both in Cuba and other countries, this information will refer to the non-Cuban cigar) followed by the specifics on the actual cigars that we smoked. Following each heading, you'll find symbols that classify each cigar. The first classification is price; the symbols I've used indicate a general price range for the brand of cigar and the styles available ($4 and under, $; $4 to $7, $$; $7 to $10, $$$; $10 and over, $$$$). Cigar prices vary across the country due to many factors (the high taxes imposed on cigars being one of the major ones). Because of this, you may find some cigars falling outside of the ranges published here.

The second classification is by country. Keep in mind that this is only an indication of the country of manufacture and what can generally be expected from cigars made in this country. Although a cigar might be manufactured in the Dominican Republic, if it sports a Cameroon wrapper, a Mexican binder and a filler composed of tobaccos from the Dominican Republic and several other countries, it will taste vastly different from one that has primarily Dominican Republic tobaccos. Where possible, I've included information on the particular elements of various cigars; however, these elements can (and do) change, and it can all be somewhat confusing, especially if you're just starting out, so these descriptions are fairly general. When you get to the point where you want to learn more about a specific cigar, look to see if it's been rated or tested in either *Smoke* or *Cigar Aficionado*. Both publications will have the most up-to-date manufacturing information.

Finally, you'll see an indication of the cigar's strength, ranging from mild to full. Keep in mind that this is only an indication. I haven't read a cigar review or rating yet that didn't contradict itself when more than one person was consulted. I've tried to balance the different opinions I received on these cigars as much as possible, but it's difficult to do when one person ranks a cigar as medium strength and the next person finds it mild.

I've also singled out a few cigars as top picks, based on a number of factors such as consistency, construction, price, and general smoking pleasure among them.

May you have as much fun on your personal journey through cigars as I have.

Arturo Fuente $–$$$$ Dominican Republic
Medium to full

The Fuente family is the second largest producer of handmade cigars in the Dominican Republic, so you'd think their cigars would be easy to come by. Wrong! For a variety of reasons, they've become immensely popular in the last year or so and have been very difficult to find. At the time of this writing, the Fuente factories were struggling to fill a multiyear backlog of orders and were accepting no new orders or accounts. Although the family has stated that it intends to increase production in coming years, it may take a year or two for them to come even remotely close to filling the demand for these cigars.

When I first started writing this book, however, a number of Fuente styles were still readily available, and I loved every Fuente I tried, finding them handsome cigars with smooth, almost matte wrappers, very aromatic and cedary smelling. Most of the Fuentes I smoked had maduro wrappers because that's what I preferred at the time, and to me they were the epitome of what a maduro-wrapped cigar should taste like.

As much as I have enjoyed these cigars, I declined to designate them a top pick for a couple of reasons. First off, they're too hard to come by, and why set people up for a fall when they just aren't available? Secondly, their immense popularity has driven their price up beyond what many feel is a good value for this cigar. So, should you seek them out? Absolutely, but don't be disappointed if you can't find them. When you do, you may have to decide if they're worth the price. When you do see them at a tobacconist, don't be surprised if your purchase is limited to a handful.

I've also hesitated on recommending any particular styles, again because they're so difficult to come by. In going back over my tasting notes on these cigars, I consistently gave them high marks, particularly the funny little Hemingway Short Story (a baby perfecto) and the Chateau Fuente, a tasty, cedar-wrapped 4 ½", 50-ring robusto that I went back to time and time again. But I also enjoyed the cheap little medium-filler Fuente curlyhead that a friend gave me out of his personal stash. So, again, if you see them, buy them, especially if you find them in a size you enjoy smoking.

The Fuente family is also the manufacturer of the much-lauded Opus X series, the first Dominican Republic cigar made with all

Dominican tobacco. A truly magnificent cigar, the Opus X is felt by many to be the rare cigar that deserves its hype as well as its price. If you're lucky enough to find one, be prepared to pay a lot for it; prices $15 and up are not uncommon. And be prepared to be limited to a purchase of two or three.

Ashton $–$$$$ Dominican Republic
Mild to medium

Ashtons hail from the Dominican Republic and are made in three different lines, each with its own style of flavor. All three are wrapped in Connecticut leaf; the Ashton Aged Maduro line gets a Connecticut broadleaf wrapper instead of shade.

Of the three, I particularly enjoy the Cabinet Selection. It has the most flavor and body, and is also the most expensive, owing to extra aging of the tobaccos used to make it. I enjoyed the No. 3 in this line, which is a 6", 46-ring grand corona, finding it an exceptionally pleasant, easy-smoking cigar, with a nicely balanced, nutty/cedary flavor, and an even, smooth draw. For a mild to medium smoke in the medium price range, go for anything in the standard selection; I especially like the 5 ½", 44-ring corona. The Aged Maduro line is also a good choice if you like a maduro wrapper; they can also be somewhat hard to find. They're fuller-bodied with a great chocolately taste.

Astral $$–$$$ Honduras   Mild to medium

This relatively new brand is a light-bodied Honduran with a smooth, creamy flavor. I found it a nicely balanced smoke, lighter than many Hondurans, and one that I would recommend to anyone if they were a little up in the air about what they liked to smoke. Try the Beso if you like a robusto length; I also like the 6 ½", 44-ring Lujos.

Avo $$–$$$ Dominican Republic   Mild to medium

A smooth Dominican cigar with a handsome, leather-colored wrapper. Actual smoking experiences with these were mixed due to storage and construction problems—the pyramid I tried split on me, and the Preludio, a corona, was a tight, tight, tight draw—but the way these cigars tasted was worth the problems. Two different series: the standard selection sports a light peach band; the XO comes with more of a pink-colored band and is said to have a bit more complex of a fill as well as a unique aging and fermenting process. It is also more expensive. I found the bigger-ring Avos better than the narrower ones, with a richer, more complex flavor. Largely due to its price, this is a cigar I reserve for special occasions. I thought it was perfect following a roast beef dinner.

What is a plugged cigar?

If it feels like you're busting a lung or two when you're drawing on a cigar, chances are that cigar is plugged. This can happen with a cigar that has been rolled too tightly or with one that has been over-humidified, which can also make a cigar difficult to draw on. Cigars made with maduro wrappers can be difficult draws.

There's not much you can do with a plugged cigar. If it's truly an unbearable smoke, put it down and try a new cigar. Some tobacconists sell a plastic tool that basically pokes a hole through the length of the body of the cigar, which may help the draw. You can use a bamboo skewer for the same affect.

Baccarat $ Honduras   Mild to medium

These are well-priced cigars with just a touch of spiciness. They aren't the most exciting cigar out there, but not a bad choice for an everyday smoke and they're a decent buy for the money. Don't be surprised by the hint of sugar on your tongue when you go to light one of these up. The manufacturer uses a specially sweetened gum to seal the cigar's cap. Several styles are also available in a maduro wrapper. Although Baccarats come in a wide range of sizes, I prefer the smaller ones, such as the 6", 43-ring Luchadores and the 5", 50-ring Rothschild.

Bering $ Honduras   Medium

Bering is one of the better drug store brands you can buy for a quick, cheap smoke, and their premium line is also a good buy. These are really decent cigars for the money; I don't think I've ever paid much over $2 for any of them. They have somewhat of an earthy, woodsy taste to them, and a full, classic cigar aroma. They're an outdoor stadium type of cigar—if you can find one that still allows cigar smoking, that is. The 6 ¼", 46-ring corona grande is one of my old standbys, but there are some nine or ten other styles available.

TOP PICK
Butera Royal Vintage $$–$$$
Dominican Republic   Mild

Mike Butera of the Butera Pipe Company is the force behind these very popular and often hard-to-get cigars. This Dominican cigar is very smooth with lots of flavor, enhanced by Butera's special aging process that involves curing the cigars under a bed of moistened cedar chips.

Sometimes you'll hear people describe cigars as buttery or creamy; the Butera is the epitome of these adjectives. It sports one of the world's prettiest wrappers, too, the color of milk caramel with a pleasant, nutty/cedary aroma. Try the Bravo Corto, a 4 ½", 50-ring robusto, the Cedro Fino, a 6 ½", 4 ½" ring Lonsdale, or the Dorado 652, a 6", 52-ring toro.

The Butera Royal Vintage cigars rated a top pick, albeit somewhat grudgingly, because they're a little pricey. But all the people who smoked them ended up wishing they had more of these wonderful cigars, and if they smoked the robusto length, they wished they had a longer one. Personally, I would not choose these cigars for an everyday smoke, even if I could afford them. They're too special to be turned into a pedestrian experience.

Canaria D'Oro $ Dominican Republic
Mild to medium

This Dominican has a nice flavor with just a hint of sweetness and spice. Although made in the Dominican Republic, they are primarily Mexican, with some Dominican and Jamaican tobacco used in the filler. Priced well, they appeal to anyone wanting a smooth but well-bodied smoke at a good price. Try the 4 ½", 50-ring Rothschild; the Babies at just over 4" and with a 32-ring is a good quick smoke.

CAO $$–$$$ Honduras   Mild to medium

An incredibly good-looking cigar—the maduros are especially handsome with their dark wrappers and white ash—the CAO is a cigar I would smoke while out at a bar or at dinner. They have a nice, balanced fragrance, a smooth, even wrapper, and a very elegant appearance. The 6", 50-ring Corona Gorda maduro was consistently a smooth, mellow smoke, although a bit of a hard draw due to its tight pack.

Capellan $$–$$$ Dominican Republic
Medium to full

A relative newcomer, this Dominican cigar sports a somewhat oily, medium-brown wrapper and is very consistent in construction and flavor. These cigars pack a lot of smoke and will fill a room with their aroma. Full-bodied but smooth with just a touch of spice, this is one for the heavy hitters at the board meeting.

Carlin $–$$ **Dominican Republic**   **Medium**

The Carlin, made in the Dominican Republic, is a medium-bodied cigar with a finish that people describe as being anywhere from chocolatey to coffee-flavored. Their Colorado maduro wrappers give them a somewhat sweet taste. Recommended: the 5 ½", 43-ring corona, a nice choice for anyone desiring a smaller ring size than a robusto or toro.

Carlos Torano $$–$$$ **Dominican Republic**
Mild to medium

These cigars sport a light, elegant claro wrapper and have a bit of a spicy or peppery taste. They're not one I'd smoke during the day, but were pretty nice paired with a peaty single-malt Scotch in the evening.

Credo $$–$$$ **Dominican Republic**
Mild to medium

These Dominican cigars with the familiar name (yes, there is a tie to the famous Credo humidifying device here) come in some of the most elegant, understated boxes I've ever seen. The cigar tends toward the elegant side as well, at least in appearance. It's somewhat of an unusual smoke; its appearance leads you expect it to be mild and smooth, but it turns out to be more rugged than that. I liked this cigar for after dinner, and enjoyed it several times with cognac. Try the almost 7", 46-ring Magnificat or the Arcane, a robusto.

Cruz Real $$ **Mexico**   **Medium**

This Mexican cigar is often described as rustic-tasting, and I completely agree with that description. It can be spicy and somewhat dry to the taste. It comes in both Colorado claro and maduro wrappers; the maduro I tried was almost unbearably spicy and had almost an earthy taste to it.

Cubita $$–$$$ Dominican Republic   Full

These cigars look like they'd be full and heady, and they are. They're spicy, earthy, and fragrant; most people smell cedar when they're burning, but I've also heard them described as chocolately. A great choice for after a cigar dinner or with your favorite full-bodied wine. The 7", 50-ring #2000 is a good smoke if you have the requisite time to finish it.

**Cuesta Rey $–$$$$
United States, Dominican Republic   Mild to medium**

This old brand was one of many that moved to the United States, specifically, Ybor City near Tampa, Florida, in the late 1890s. Today, the standard Cuesta Rey is still machine-made in Tampa; the company's long-filler cigars are made in the Dominican Republic. There are three different Cuesta Rey lines: the machine-made Cuesta Rey, the Cabinet Selection, and the Centennial Collection. These cigars tend to have a sweet, mild flavor, which reminds some smokers of cloves. The Cabinet Selection is fuller-bodied, but still retains the sweetness and clove fragrance.

**Daniel Marshall $$–$$$
Dominican Republic, Honduras   Medium**

Daniel Marshall makes some of the most beautiful humidors in the world, much prized among celebrity cigar smokers who can well afford the price these babies command. His name is also on some very handsome cigars that sport some of the more elegant bands in the business. Two blends are available: Dominican and Honduran. Although both are worth trying, the Honduran is fuller-bodied and has a more complex blend of tobacco of the two, and it's also more expensive. When I first heard about these cigars, I didn't believe the hype, but when I got around to smoking the one I had in my humidor, I was sorry I hadn't bought more. Although priced a bit high to rank as an everyday smoke, they're good enough to want to smoke often. Definitely worth looking for.

Don Jose $ Honduras   Medium

I was given one of these inexpensive Honduran cigars by a friend and found it to be a nice surprise with a rich, yet smooth flavor, so I bought some of my own. They come in both natural and maduro wrappers; the maduro makes the cigar a little fuller in body and gives it a slight cocoa taste. Definitely worth trying if you're looking for a cheap everyday cigar with a little more character than many.

Don Juan $ Nicaragua   Mild

These Nicaraguan cigars are pretty mild and a good deal for the price. If you're looking for a big, impressive cigar that won't overpower you, Don Juan's Presidente is a good pick at 8 ½" and with a 50 ring.

Don Tomas $–$$ Honduras   Medium

A well-constructed Honduran with three lines at differing price levels. The Special Edition sports a Connecticut shade wrapper and tends to be a bit milder than the International and Standard series. I especially liked the robusto size in the Special Edition, but I also enjoyed all the Don Tomas cigars that I smoked. Well worth seeking out as they're well-priced, well-constructed, very smokable cigars.

Dunhill Aged Cigars $$–$$$
Dominican Republic   Mild to medium

The venerable Dunhill name appears on three lines of cigars available in the United States: the Aged Cigar, produced in the Dominican Republic, the Dunhill, produced in the Canary Islands, and the Dunhill Small Cigars, a dry cigar made in Holland. I really enjoyed the 6", 48-ring Aged Condado that I smoked with its pleasant, cedary aroma and nutty flavor.

El Incomparable $$$–$$$$
Dominican Republic   Mild to medium

These premium cigars come in a creamy yellow, cedar-lined tube. Unscrew the top, and the unmistakable aroma of Scotch instantly wafts its way to your awaiting nostrils. Seeped in Springbank, a single-malt Scotch, these cigars are wonderfully good and well worth their premium pricing. Definitely not an everyday smoke, but a wonderful choice for a celebration. Many tasters found these a somewhat tight draw, but worth the effort. The draw seems to be better on the robusto length, which are also somewhat difficult to find.

El Rey Del Mundo $$–$$$ Honduras
Medium to full

El Rey Del Mundo means *the king of the world* in Spanish. I'm not sure the cigars entirely live up to this lofty name, but I did like them, especially the Flor de LaVonda, a 6 ½", 52-ring pyramid. They were very robust and a little harsh at the beginning, but became immensely better as they were smoked.

El Rico Habano $–$$ United States
Medium to full

This is the sister (brother?) brand to the La Gloria Cubana, made at the same factory in Florida with Honduran, Nicaraguan, and Ecuadorian tobaccos. These cigars have a smooth, almost silky wrapper and a great aroma. Although I liked them, I found them a somewhat harsh smoke at first, but they grew smoother and fuller-bodied as I kept at it.

El Sublimado $$$–$$$$
Dominican Republic   Mild

The sister brand to the El Incomparable, the El Sublimado is steeped in fifty-year-old Noces d'Or cognac. Again, this is not an everyday cigar, but one to consider for a special occasion. I found the cognac aroma to be a bit cloying when I first opened the tube, but it dissipated somewhat while I smoked it, and I ended up enjoying this cigar nearly as much as the El Incomparable.

Europa $ United States   Full

These 5 ½", 34-ring cheroots are kinda cute, if that word can be used to describe a cigar. They sport a very rough, veiny wrapper that tastes like it's been dipped in something sweet. I picked this one up at a tobacconist in Minneapolis as a recommendation for a full-bodied cigar, which it definitely is. It's also an inexpensive, machine-made U.S. cigar, and a good quick-and-dirty evening smoke. People might look at you funny if you smoke it in other places than your own home as it does look a bit like a twig.

Excalibur by Hoyo de Monterrey $$–$$$
Honduras   Medium to full

The Excalibur No. 1 was one of the cigars (along with the Ashton) that ushered in my return to cigar smoking, and the first cigar I felt strongly enough about to buy a whole box of. Available in nine sizes, ranging from the 3", 22-ring Miniature to the 7 ¼", 54-ring No. 1 (my favorite). Available in natural and maduro wrappers, these cigars are an excellent choice for anyone looking for a robust, well-constructed, top-end cigar at a reasonable price. Some think these are the best non-Cuban cigars on the market.

Felipe Gregorio $$–$$$ **Honduras**   **Medium**

This Honduran cigar has a peppery-colored, silky wrapper paired with a handsome, regal band. I found them to be rich cigars with a very fragrant aroma. Their somewhat heavy construction made them feel very substantial in my hand, and several of them were a somewhat tight draw. They are especially enjoyable after a good meal and as a late-night smoke with a snifter of cognac.

TOP PICK
Fonseca $–$$$
Dominican Republic   **Mild to medium**

I think these cigars are somewhat overlooked by many cigar smokers, and there's a part of me that hopes they'll continue to be, so their prices stay on the reasonable side. They are wonderfully smooth Dominican cigars that sport either a Connecticut shade, or in the case of the maduros, a broadleaf wrapper. They are very consistent in construction and character, and well-priced for what you get. Every one of them is worth trying; I'm particularly fond of the 2-2, a petit corona; the 7-9-9, a grand corona, and the Pyramid, a triangular that delivers a very rich taste. The maduros can be very hard to find.

The Griffin's $$–$$$ **Dominican Republic**
Mild to medium

Produced and marketed by Davidoff, these are very attractive cigars with a caramel-colored Connecticut wrapper and very clean construction. They have a somewhat woodsy aroma and a pleasant, slightly spicy taste. Their consistency in construction and taste makes them a good, everyday cigar (although a bit pricey for some); they're also a good choice if you need to buy a gift for a friend but you're not quite sure what he or she likes to smoke. I liked the No. 500, a 5", 43-ring corona.

H. Upmann $$–$$$ Dominican Republic
Mild to medium

These legendary cigars originated in Cuba in the mid-1800s; to-day, they hail from the Dominican Republic as well.

All the Upmanns I tried were somewhat sweet and full-flavored with somewhat oily Colorado maduro wrappers. I especially liked the Pequenos No. 100, a 4 ½", 50-ring robusto.

Habana Gold $$–$$$ Honduras   Mild to medium

There are two Habana Gold lines. They're both made in Honduras, but they're constructed from tobacco hailing from other countries as well. The major difference between the two is their wrappers: the Black Label sports an Ecuadorian wrapper, and the White Label is wrapped in Nicaraguan tobacco. The ones I smoked in both lines were uneven in construction and I found several to be very hard draws.

Henry Clay $–$$ Dominican Republic
Medium to full

Named after the American senator with business interests in Cuba, this medium- to full-bodied cigar was produced in Cuba for many years, moving to Trenton, New Jersey, in the 1930s and then to the Dominican Republic. They sport a dark, oily wrapper and an appearance and fragrance that has often been described as rustic. They're not for everyone, but worth trying if you like a full-bodied cigar at a reasonable price.

Joya de Nicaragua $ Nicaragua   Mild to medium

The quality of these cigars has been a bit up and down due to the turmoil in Nicaragua, but they are certainly worth a try as they are reasonably priced and deliver a good, mild flavor with the hint of sweetness that is characteristic of many Nicaraguan cigars. Available in both natural and maduro wrappers. The 4 ½", 52-ring Consul is a great everyday smoke if you can find them.

La Aurora $ Dominican Republic
Mild to medium

I found these Dominican cigars on the mild side without a great deal of body, but others rated them as more medium-bodied—I think because they also have a spicy aroma. An enjoyable cigar for the money.

La Gloria Cubana $–$$ United States
Medium to full

As you progress in your enjoyment of cigars, and especially if you spend any time researching them on-line, you'll read a lot about these cigars, which are the American version of a Havana cigar made in Miami by Ernesto Carillo. Some hail these cigars as the best thing they've ever smoked; others will tell you they're way overhyped and not worth the money, even though they aren't very expensive . . . yet.

What is true about these cigars is that they tend to be shipped green, therefore benefiting greatly by aging prior to smoking—or at least, this is what I've always read about them. Being somewhat of a natural skeptic (and also an impatient sort at times), I bought several LGC Wavells when they appeared at a local tobacconist and immediately smoked one. It was absolutely awful! I threw the last two into the deep recesses of my humidor, where they resided for three months while I forgot about them. By the time I retrieved them, one of them smoked wonderfully; the other was still green-tasting and harsh, and I was sorry I hadn't let it sit longer. But that's the problem with these cigars. I've heard lots of people sing the praises of the Churchills and the torpedos; I like the Wavell, a 5", 50-ring robusto.

Due to the demand for these cigars, some are now being produced in the Dominican Republic as well.

La Unica $–$$ Dominican Republic   Medium

These bundle Dominican cigars are not as cheap as they used to be, but still a good buy for a decent, everyday smoke. They come in both natural and maduro wrappers.

Macanudo $$–$$$$
Dominican Republic, Jamaica   Mild to medium

Consistency, consistency, consistency. This is what you'll find with Macanudo. These are handsome, very well-made cigars, which provide one of the very best smooth, mild smokes on the market.

Macanudos come in a variety of sizes, some of which offer a choice of wrapper color as well. Most of the ones you'll see will be the cafe style, a very attractive cigar made with Connecticut shade wrappers; there's also a jade, which is a greenish, double claro wrapper. Some styles also come in a maduro wrapper hailing from Mexico. There is also a vintage cabinet selection, which is more expensive and fuller-bodied than the standard line.

These cigars are excellent daytime smokes and are also enjoyable after a light meal. They are some of my favorite cigars for smoking when I'm out in public and not entirely sure I'm in an establishment that allows cigar smoking. The Miniatures, in fact, will often escape detection even by the most sensitive nostrils. They're also one of my favorite brands for handing to women who really aren't sure they'd like a cigar, but are game to give it a try anyway.

Madrigal $–$$ Mexico   Mild

This Mexican cigar has somewhat of a vegetal smell, a pretty band, and the ugliest ash I've ever seen. It was a surprisingly nice smoke, with more flavor than I've experienced with other Mexican cigars.

MiCubano $–$$ Nicaragua   Full

An all-Nicaraguan cigar made up of 100 percent Cuban-seed tobacco. This is a cigar that packs a wallop, perhaps too strong for many people; however, anyone looking for a rich, full-bodied cigar should take a look at these. Try the No. 450, a 4 ¾", 50-ring robusto, or the No. 542, a 5 ½", 42-ring corona.

**Montecristo $$–$$$ Dominican Republic
Medium**

If you like medium-bodied cigars, these are definitely a brand to try. Although I found selection somewhat limited, the Montecristos I smoked were consistently well-made, with somewhat of a cocoa flavor and a little spice.

**Montecruz $–$$ Dominican Republic
Mild to medium**

Another one of the M cigars from the Dominican Republic, this is a pleasant cigar that is often described as nutty or spicy.

Muniemaker $–$$ United States   Medium to full

An inexpensive, machine-made cigar with big, robust flavor. They sport a very oily maduro wrapper and they're a bit squishy feeling, but they have a good burn and draw and a very nice flavor. The wrappers on these tasted a bit salty at times.

**Nat Sherman $$–$$$ Dominican Republic
Mild to medium**

The Nat Sherman store, located at 500 Fifth Avenue in New York City, is a famous Manhattan landmark. Revered as the "Tobacconist to the World," it's an interesting and fun stop if you find yourself in New York for any reason.

I smoked a great cigar last night; this morning my mouth feels awful and my breath is horrendous. What can I do to eliminate it?

I used to think cigar breath was related to the strength of the cigar I was smoking, but that doesn't seem to be true, as I've smoked some pretty heavy cigars that didn't leave much of an aftertaste in my mouth at all. The only reasonable explanation I could come up with for this is that it may be related more to other factors—time of day, what you've eaten that day, how much you've had to drink, and what you've had to drink, whatever.

I think the easiest solution for cigar breath is to make sure that you hang out with someone who either smokes along with you or doesn't care what you smell like when you do. It's kind of like living with a garlic lover. Barring that, here are a few things to try:

1. *Breath mints.* There's a mint called Altoids that has long been favored by cigarette smokers. It's an unsweetened peppermint that really does refresh the mouth. Other mints I've tried seem to have little effect. Same thing goes for gum, which, in my experience, makes it worse.

2. *Water or iced tea.* Keeping your mouth and throat moist while smoking seems to hamper cigar breath. Supposedly, the Cubans drink very strong tea, either hot or iced, or very strong coffee, to offset the breath of a stale cigar. It's worth a shot.

3. *Toothpaste with baking soda and peroxide.* Baking soda is a natural deodorizer; peroxide is a cleanser. Brush thoroughly, more than once. Brush your tongue, too.

Nat Sherman produces a number of different lines of cigars, all made in the Dominican Republic but with different blends. I tried the City Desk Tribune, a hefty 7 ¼", 50-ring cigar with a beautiful, chocolate-brown maduro wrapper that was one of the most elegant-looking cigars I've ever smoked. Although I liked the cigar while I smoked it, it left me with an almost metallic aftertaste that lingered well into the next day.

Onyx $$–$$$ Dominican Republic   Mild

These Dominican cigars are aptly named as they sport the darkest wrappers on the market. This is an all-maduro line, with a mild taste and some spiciness. The No. 750, a 7 ½", 50-ring double corona was a winner, although some smokers felt it tasted a little green.

Ornelas $–$$$ Mexico   Mild to medium

If you're fond of vanilla, try one of the vanilla-steeped cigars in this line, which pay tribute to the early days of cigar shipping when a fresh vanilla bean was added to sweeten the pig's bladder that the cigars were packed in. There's also a cognac-steeped Ornelas for those with a little more sophisticated taste.

Padron $–$$$$ Nicaragua   Medium

These earthy cigars have some spice to them that makes them a little too much for my palate, but many other smokers really like them. The Padron Anniversary Series is very highly regarded and significantly more expensive.

Partagas $$–$$$$ Dominican Republic   Medium

Partagas is the sister cigar to Macanudo, and contains the same tobaccos in its filler, albeit in different blends, that distinguish these cigars from their milder-flavored kin. These cigars are almost as consistent as the Macanudo as well, and are noted for their classic, spicy aroma and smooth, yet full taste.

The Partagas name is also on some of the nicest and most expensive cigars I've ever smoked: the Partagas 150 Signature Series. Introduced in 1995, a limited number were made, and most of them were instantly purchased, making these cigars instantly scarce and very expensive. However, there's something of a secondary market in these cigars, so you may see them pop up on occasion at your local tobacconist. With their specially aged Cameroon wrappers, they are a wonderful smoke, smooth, medium-bodied, and slightly sweet; one that, for me, is definitely worth the $18 to $22 I have paid for the larger sizes.

Paul Gamirian   **$$–$$$**
Dominican Republic   **Medium**

Cigar aficionado Paul Gamirian, author of *The Gourmet Guide to Cigars*, launched the line of cigars carrying his name in 1991. They're well-made with very even construction, and they come in a broad range of sizes. These Dominican Republic cigars are on the fuller-bodied side, and I found them somewhat spicy as well. They sport a very attractive, reddish brown wrapper that almost seems color coordinated with their gold and red bands. A good after-dinner or late-evening smoke.

TOP PICK
Petrus   **$–$$$**   **Honduras**
Mild to medium

Consistency and value make these cigars a top pick. I loved every Petrus I tried, finding them a nicely balanced, smooth smoke with a slightly sweet finish. Available in both natural and maduro wrappers.

Pleiades   **$$–$$$**   **Dominican Republic**   **Mild**

I was given a Pleiades cigar for my birthday about a year ago, and was intrigued by its elegant, almost fragile-appearing wrapper and thin, understated band.

This is a very mild cigar, made in the Caribbean with a very light Connecticut shade wrapper. Interestingly, after the cigars are manufactured, they are shipped to France, where they are packaged in boxes with a special, built-in humidification device before being shipped back across the ocean. Each style is named after a constellation or a planet.

TOP PICK
Punch $–$$$ Honduras   Medium to full

A well-known Havana brand (and one that packs quite a wallop), the Honduran Punch brand comes in three series: Standard, Delux, and Gran Cru. They are made by the same company as the Hoyo de Monterrey and there are definitely similarities between the two brands.

The standard line offers a very well-priced Rothschild size that I am particularly fond of. I found the Gran Crus that I tried to be somewhat harsh when first lit, but they became more flavorful as they went on.

TOP PICK
**Puros Indios $–$$$$ Honduras
Medium to full**

These are exceptional cigars and another top pick, based on price, construction, and pure smoking satisfaction. Every Puros Indios I smoked was consistent in flavor and construction; however, recent shipments have been a little green and very densely packed, necessitating more lung power than I sometimes felt should be necessary to yield a good amount of smoke. This cigar is made with an interesting blend of Brazilian, Dominican, and Nicaraguan tobacco and sport Ecuadorian wrappers. They're available in a large range of sizes; the Petit Perla (a short panatela) is usually a good buy. If you're looking for a long cigar, the 18" General is one of the longest regular-production cigars around.

Royal Jamaica $–$$ Dominican Republic   Mild

This is a popular low-priced cigar, which, contrary to its name, is actually made in the Dominican Republic with Jamaican filler. Although a mild cigar, expect some spiciness in the wrapper.

Santa Rosa $–$$ Honduras   Mild to medium

I loved these Honduran cigars, with their almost peanutty aroma and salty-tasting Connecticut shade wrappers. The last time I smoked one was over an impromptu pool game; they seem to suit this sort of activity.

Te Amo $–$$ Mexico   Mild to medium

People either love or hate Mexican cigars; there's very little middle ground when it comes to them. The Te Amo was the first Mexican cigar I tried, and I approached it with some hesitation, knowing its black-and-white history. It wasn't the worst cigar I'd ever had, but it wasn't the best, with somewhat of an earthy, peppery taste and vegetal fragrance. However, it did mellow out and get better as I smoked it, which I've heard the Te Amo tends to do. For me, the jury is still out on these. Try one yourself and see what side of the fence you land on.

Temple Hall $–$$$ Jamaica   Medium

Although Jamaican cigars have the reputation of being mild, the Temple Hall is anything but with its combination of Jamaican, Dominican, and Mexican tobaccos. This is a reintroduction of a venerable old brand that's been around since 1876, and it's worth looking for and trying. I liked the No. 700, a 7", 49-ring double corona.

Thomas Hinds $$–$$$ Nicaragua, Honduras   Medium

If it has a green band, it's a Thomas Hinds Honduran Selection; the white bands hail from Nicaragua. The Honduran Selection is strong but not ridiculously so; pair it with your favorite after-dinner drink for a relaxing evening. The Nicaraguan blend comes in both a natural wrapper and a very flavorful aged maduro; I especially liked the Lonsdale in this blend, although it had almost a vegetal smell at first.

Zino $–$$$$ Honduras   Mild to medium

This Honduran line is named after the late Zino Davidoff, and it offers a variety of cigars that are all pretty decent. A cigarette-smoking friend of mine is particularly fond of the Zino Princesse, a gold-banded cigarillo in the standard line that she has no trouble inhaling until I remind her she shouldn't. The Mouton Cadet series, which sport wine-colored bands, tend to be fuller-bodied; I particularly liked the No. 6, a rich, aromatic robusto.

Davidoff also makes a number of machine-made cigars under the Zino label. Two that I've tried are the Classic Brasil and the Classic Sumatra. Both are 4 ¾", 41-ring petit coronas. I found them both so-so, but they're reasonably priced and convenient as they come precut and in a humidor pack that supposedly keeps them fresh.

A WORD ABOUT CUBAN CIGARS

Maybe, just maybe, the United States' trade embargo against Cuba will be lifted in our lifetime, enabling us all the pleasures associated with the legendary brands of Havana.

However, until this does happen, importing, possessing, and smoking Cuban cigars is illegal for U.S. citizens. This doesn't mean you can go to a foreign country and legally indulge, either; the law applies whether you're in the United States or not. (The chances of you being caught and prosecuted in a foreign country, however, seem rather slim.)

Any U.S. citizen caught consorting with a legendary Cuban in his or her hand runs the risk of paying a $50,000 fine, imprisonment of not more than ten years, or both. The only current exception to this is for cigars brought in by individuals such as diplomatic officials, journalists, and the like returning from an official visit to Cuba. And even these select few are limited to bringing back just $100 worth of cigars. That's usually just a handful.

Although Cuban cigars are illegal in the United States, that doesn't mean there aren't any in this country and that they aren't available. Illegal Cuban cigars enter the country in various ways. Some are smuggled in by travelers to overseas countries or to Canada and Mexico. Others are shipped in by various methods. Once in this country, possession is rarely prosecuted. In fact, I have yet to hear of anyone being charged with possession of illegal cigars.

What regularly does happen, however, is that the offending contraband is confiscated by customs officials when discovered in the belongings of travelers returning to the United States, at great embarrassment (and loss) to the unlucky cigar-lover. Some people try to avoid this by taking the bands off the cigars they are trying to bring in and by putting the cigars into a box from another country; however, when in doubt, customs officials seize first and ask questions later. (The customs officials are supposed to destroy any contraband they seize, but they tend to be rather noncommittal when questioned on this.) Civil fines, which can be steep, can also be levied.

Celebrities such as Arnold Schwarzenegger and David Letterman are legendary Cuban cigar aficionados. Go into any tobacconist with a keep—special, private humidors that customers may rent or purchase for cigar storage—and I guarantee there will be some Cuban Punches, Montecristos, Cohibas, Hoyo de Monterreys, or Partagas behind locked doors. But the tobacconist won't know a thing about them. Cubans hold a powerful allure, they are routinely rated in both of the leading cigar magazines, and there will probably come a time when you'll want to try one or two (or more).

As a group, Cuban cigars have a reputation as intense, full-bodied, heady smokes. However, not all are. They do have a definable taste and aroma that mark them as what they are, but some of them can actually be on the mild side. Several Hoyo de Monterreys that I've had definitely fell into this category.

A friend just came back from Mexico, boasting to the immediate world of his incredible find—a box of Cohibas for $50! From what I've read, they're most likely counterfeit. Should I burst his bubble, or let him believe he got the deal of the century?

It depends on how good a friend he is. But you're right, they're more than likely counterfeit. Think about it for a minute. Real, legitimate Cohibas purchased overseas go for $10 or more per cigar. Why then, would he be able to find a whole box of them for $50 in Mexico? Makes sense, doesn't it! If you want to let him down gently, tell him what you just read. If he's got any sense at all, he'll realize what he did and shut up.

Although it varies at times, the legendary brands such as Punch, Partagas, Hoyo de Monterrey, Montecristo, and Cohiba seem to be most available. Be aware that many of these brands are being rushed to market due to the incredible demand for them, and they may be too young to enjoyably smoke. The quality may be uneven, and the construction perhaps poorer than what you may be accustomed to if you've been smoking premium cigars from other countries. Again, this is largely due to demand.

If you routinely check on-line services or the Internet, you'll see Cuban cigars being offered for sale. Although no one's quite sure of the monitoring of the airwaves, remember that anything posted on a bulletin board or public access area means exactly that—it's not just for your eyes only. If you're offered Cuban cigars in the United States or Mexico for what seems to be an incredibly good price, beware. They're most assuredly fake. Mexico is notorious for producing Cuban knockoffs.

Both *Cigar Aficionado* and *Smoke* routinely include Cuban cigars in their ratings and tastings sections, and they're good resources for learning more about specific Cuban brands and styles. *Cigar Aficionado* also publishes a Cuban cigar guide that compiles the ratings for all the cigars it has profiled. For a most complete compilation, check out *Perelman's Pocket Cyclopedia for Cuban Cigars.*

I just received a box of Cuban cigars from a friend. With all the counterfeit cigars around today, how can I tell if they're real Cubans?

For starters, the label sealing the box should be green and white (a custom dating from 1912), and should read "Cuban Government's warranty for cigars exported from Havana. Republica de Cuba. Sello de garantia nacional de procedencia."

Hecho en Cuba has been stamped on the underside of Cuban boxes since 1961, when it replaced the English inscription "Made in Havana—Cuba." In 1989, the words "Totalmente a Mano" were added, which mean "totally by hand." Cigars manufactured prior to 1994 will have a Cubatabaco logo; it was replaced in late 1994 with the Habanos S.A. logo.

Cigars manufactured in Cuba since 1985 also carry a factory code, stamped in blue and using the initials of the postrevolutionary factory names. JM stands for Jose Marti (formerly H. Upmann), FPG stands for Francisco Perez German (formerly Partagas), BM stands for Briones Montoto (formerly Romeo y Julieta), FR stands for Fernando Roig (formerly La Corona), and HM stands for Heroes del Moncada (formerly El Rey del Mundo). Boxes stamped with EL stands for El Laguito, a manufacturing facility started in postrevolutionary Cuba.

Tip-offs that the box of Cuban cigars you are holding might be fake are subtle variations in the way the band or the Cuban guarantee label is printed. Sometimes, the only way to tell whether a Cuban cigar is fake or not is to smoke it and let your taste buds be your guide. There's no way to duplicate the look and taste of an actual Cuban cigar, although you may not possess the frame of reference upon which to base this comparison.

CIGARS FOR A SPECIAL OCCASION

El Incomparable
La Sublimado
Butera Royal Vintage
Avo XO
Felipe Gregorio

IF YOU LIKE MADUROS

Joya de Nicaragua
Onyx
Henry Clay
Hoyo de Monterrey
Punch
Ashton
Puros Indios
CAO
Don Tomas
Petrus
T. Hinds Nicaraguan Selection
MiCubano

ALL-AROUND EVERYDAY SMOKES

Carlin
Royal Jamaica
Don Tomas
Baccarat
Fonseca
Joya de Nicaragua
Punch Rothschild

8

Resources

Cigar smoking's popularity has spawned a host of books, magazines, newsletters, videos, and information in other formats as well. While doing the research for this book, I waded through more than I ever dreamed was written about tobacco and cigars, watched a few videotapes, and surfed the Web more than once. By the time these words reach you, there will be even more information on cigars for you to choose from.

Much of what I've listed below was used as sources of information for this book. Some was not, but all is offered for the benefit of readers wanting to know more about cigars, smoking, and the history of tobacco. Some of the older or more obscure books, such as *Holy Smoke* and Zino Davidoff's *The Connoisseur's Book of the Cigar*, are difficult to come by or out of print. However, if you live near a major library or have access to one, you should be able to locate a copy. The newer books, as well as the periodicals and videotapes, are available (or can be ordered) at most tobacconists, newsstands, and bookstores.

The Ultimate Cigar Book, by Richard Carleton Hacker, is the cigar bible for many aficionados. Hacker brings many, many years as both a smoker and a writer to this fine guide, and the width and depth of his knowledge is legendary (he has visited every cigar-producing country in the world). His international compendium of cigars, which occupies the last quarter or so of the book, is a highly sub-

131

jective review (even he says so) of hundreds of cigars—both Cuban and non—based on the Highly Prejudiced HackerScale (HPH), which rates them from 1 to 3 based on strength, rather than taste. A highly anticipated second edition was released in the fall of 1996, full of updated information and an expanded listing including cigars not available when the first edition was published in 1993. Both editions are worth owning, since the second edition amplifies but doesn't supersede the first; if you're going to build a library of books on cigars, Hacker definitely should have a place on the shelf.

An old studio still of Groucho Marx, asleep on a divan with his ever-present cigar clamped between his teeth, provides a clue as to what lurks inside the cover of *Holy Smoke*, by G. Cabrera Infante (Harper & Row, 1985). At first blush, it's a free-association ramble through cigar lore and history, full of puns, plays on words, and seemingly obscure references linking personages as diverse as vaudevillian comedians and literary greats. It's a tough read at first, but stick with it, and you'll find a funny, irreverent, and, yes, even educational romp through all things nicotiana, penned by a native Cuban blessed with a delightful command of a second language. Infante's mind is a deep and wide repository for anything remotely tobacco-related. His discussion of the role smoking has played in movies and literature is incredibly well researched and very enjoyable. You won't believe, nor will you remember, how many places a cigar has appeared until you read this book. And, by the end of the book, it all does come together and make sense.

For an excellent illustrated history on tobacco, its customs, and its influence in American history and economics, turn to *Tobacco & Americans* by Robert K. Heimann (McGraw-Hill, 1960). Heimann presents a thoroughly researched account of the early discoveries of Columbus and others and tobacco history up to 1960.

The Gentle Art of Smoking (G. P. Putnam's Sons), by legendary men's outfitter and tobacconist Alfred H. Dunhill, was written at a time (1954) when the art of enjoying premium tobacco products was on a worldwide decline and in the process of being supplanted by the convenience and price afforded by machine-made cigarettes (you can almost envision Dunhill's upper lip curl as he denounces this trend in his introduction). It was Dunhill's stated objective to try to stem this tide by offering a reeducation to those smokers who were not yet so far gone that they could not be redeemed, and to awaken a sense of adventure when it comes to enjoying tobacco products.

Whether Dunhill achieves his stated objective could be argued, and the credibility of this book suffers somewhat from some interesting inaccuracies: for example, Dunhill reverses the characteristics of tobacco leaves while on the plant (in his world, the leaves on the top are the mildest). Don't let these inaccuracies deter you; there's still good reason to read this book. Do so, and you'll feel as if you've stepped back into a gentler age, when women were women and men . . . smoked fine cigars and pipes and good cigarettes—Dunhills, of course.

Tomima Edmark is the inventive lady who devised a clever hair do dad that went on to make her a not-so-small fortune. What to do with all that money? Well, marry the man of your dreams, of course, and spend your time after a busy day at the office hanging out in your hot tub with your handsome hubby, cognac floating nearby and cigar in hand. Oh, Tomima, how I'd love your life! *Cigar Chic: A Woman's Perspective*, the very chic book she wrote in 1995, opened the doors for many women who wanted to try cigars but were afraid to do so. Although written from the feminine point of view, it's a well-researched and interesting read for both sexes.

The Connoisseur's Book of the Cigar is late, legendary cigar maker Zino Davidoff's guide for the connoisseur of the cigar. Davidoff's cigar memories begin with experiences involving such folks as Lenin, who patronized the family store when it was forced to move to Geneva from Kiev after Davidoff's family was accused of conspiring with the revolutionists. This older book shows a marked prejudice toward Cuban cigars, based on Davidoff's experiences in Cuba as a young man. But his advice on all aspects of smoking is sensible and very on-point, even to this day.

Perelman's Pocket Cyclopedia of Cigars is a complete guide to man-made and machine-made cigars available in the United States. Updated annually, this is a great resource for anyone in the process of experimenting with a variety of cigars, or for identifying that mystery cigar that you liked but forgot to make any notes on. It's reasonably priced, too. A companion to the original pocket guide, *Perelman's Pocket Cyclopedia of Havana Cigars*, was released in late 1996; it too will be updated annually.

The Cigar Companion: A Connoisseur's Guide, by Anwar Bati and Simon Chase, will definitely win the heart of any cigar smoker who likes to look at great pictures of good cigars, especially photos of Cuban cigars. Due to the professional backgrounds of both authors (both have affiliations with Hunters & Frankau, the English cigar importers with long ties to Cuba), this book shows a definite bias toward Cuban products. Much of the information included, such as how to decipher the coding on boxes of Cuban cigars to determine where the cigars were manufactured, will be helpful for people interested in buying Cuban cigars who wish to avoid buying fakes.

MAGAZINES AND OTHER PERIODICALS

With its glossy, heavy cover stock (always featuring a cigar-in-hand or-mouth celebrity), luscious photography, and advertising for all things fine in this world, *Cigar Aficionado* could be mistaken for a high-gloss lifestyle magazine for those with loads of disposable income. This is the publication that is credited with single-handedly starting the cigar renaissance in this country back in 1992 when it was first introduced; the subsequent steady increase in sales of premium handmade cigars since that time would seem to attest to the influence of the magazine. Always full of interesting lifestyle articles that range far beyond just cigars, making cigars, and smoking cigars, *CA* also includes an extensive cigar rating section (including Cubans) in each bimonthly issue (the magazine was a quarterly until early 1997).

CA also publishes two cigar-purchasing guides, one specifically covering Cuban cigars (and printed in both Spanish and English), which compile the ratings published in *CA*, as well as a very reasonably priced pocket guide that includes a handy ruler and ring gauge guide for those who like to keep track of such things.

Smoke, which debuted during the holiday season in 1995, is the young upstart competitor to *Cigar Aficionado*. Somewhat similar in content to *CA*, it's geared toward a younger, more with-it audience, and its articles definitely have an edge. You'll find reviews of cigars here, conducted by a blind panel, rather than numerical ratings. Many cigar smokers feel *Smoke*'s reviews are more informative than the ratings found in *CA* (although, as can be expected, the panelists often contradict each other), and the magazine also gives some coverage to other forms of smoking besides cigars.

Cigar Monthly is the small but mighty magazine published on the West Coast by Robert Kemp, who is also a contributor to *Smoke*. Lots of great information and articles about cigars; at $18 a year, it's a bargain. Don't miss Kemp's "Heard in the Humidor" column.

Cigar Insider, another Shanken publication, is a monthly newsletter featuring breaking news and in-depth information on the cigar industry. Definitely recommended for anyone with the need to keep in touch with the latest goings on in the cigar business.

VIDEOTAPES

For most of us, who won't get opportunity to travel to tobacco-producing countries in our lifetimes (and, frankly, we may find better things to do than tour tobacco fields if we ever do land in any of these tropical countries), videotapes provide a somewhat vicarious experience of a world that falls quite far out of the realm of most of our life experiences. You might be surprised at how informative many of the videos are. There's a certain romance to the growing of tobacco and the shaping of the products fashioned from it, and these videos do an interesting job of exposing that romantic world to their viewers. Most are available at tobacconists or can be ordered direct. You'll find ads for some of them in the publications mentioned above as well as on the World Wide Web.

Cigars: From Seed to Smoke, released in 1994, is one of the older cigar-related videos available. It features a solid, straightforward history of cigars and a tour of a tobacco plantation, as well as advice on selecting, cutting, lighting, and storing cigars.

The Art of the Cigar combines a classic-jazz soundtrack with information on how tobacco is grown and harvested and how cigars are made. Actor Paul Sorvino hosts this seventy-five-minute videotape, which also includes interviews with a host of Hollywood cigar lovers.

Finding and Enjoying Your Favorite Cigar, hosted by *Cigar Monthly* publisher and editor Robert Kemp, provides simple, straightforward advice and information on all aspects of cigar smoking. Included is advice on selecting cigars with the help of a tobacconist.

The title *Cigars! The New Rage! Your Complete Guide to the Fascinating World of Cigars* echoes the persona of very enthusiastic producer/host and disc jockey Rick Dees. Dees is somewhat preternaturally cheerful; this entertaining, humorous video featuring him offers a good blend of history and entertainment to the viewer.

CIGARS ON-LINE

Cigars have certainly occupied their rightful place in the jumble of information that is floating out there in cyberspace, with hundreds of sites now occupying space in the vast system of computers that comprise the Internet. The following list covers some of the sites where you'll find information on cigars and everything having to do with them. More sites come on-line daily, and many of the sites listed should have links to them as well.

Alt.smokers.cigars

This Usenet newsgroup is an international forum chock-full of information on all aspects of cigar smoking. You'll see cigar reviews, discussions on storage and techniques, humidors, cutters—basically, all cigar-related discussions are welcome. Because it is an international forum, you'll see information on cigars not available in the United States. Access it through the Internet.

AOL's Cigar Forum

You have to subscribe to America Online to gain access to this lively forum; in recent months, it's been about the only reason I've stayed a member. Access it through AOL's Food & Drink Network, or type Cigars at the Keyword prompt. Great discussions on a variety of topics on the message boards, as well as a ton of information (called FAQs) in the files section that has been compiled from a variety of sources. The folks who routinely post on the cigar boards are extremely knowledgeable (at least most of them are) and very willing to answer (and kindly, at that) just about any question you may have. This is one of the sites where you'll find the FAQ for calibrating hygrometers. Other FAQs get into the nitty-gritty of cigar storage, construction, health issues, and more. You'll even find one listing the 800 numbers for cigar manufacturers, distributors, and mail-order suppliers. The hosts of AOL's Cigar Forum, WINE BOSS (a.k.a. Matt Green) and

MaryApp (a.k.a. Mary Arlinghaus), are both long-time, very knowledgeable cigar smokers with great senses of humor.

Compuserve Cigar Forum

I am not a Compuserve member, so I have not visited this forum myself, but other people say good things about it. Get there by typing GO WINEFORUM—it's located in library 13 of Compuserve's Wine Forum. According to the FAQ listing discussing this forum, you'll find questions and answers discussed in the messages section, files available for downloading in the library section Cigar files, and occasional interactive conferences among the forum's members.

Cigars on the World Wide Web

Web sites featuring cigars are increasing by the day. The majority of the sites feature commercial information on cigars and cigar-related items from retailers, manufacturers, and distributors, but there's other information as well, ranging from sites developed by cigar clubs to pages designed by individual cigar lovers, some more interesting than others. Yes, this is where you'll find Cuban cigars advertised for sale, as well as just about anything else that's cigar-related that you can imagine.

The Web can be confusing, but newer Web browsers have made it easier to find what you're looking for. Try using a commercial index such as Yahoo! (www.yahoo.com) for a comprehensive search, or go directly to the sites listed below for some of the best information and links.

The Internet Cigar Group <http://www.cigargroup.com> maintains some of the best information available on the Web. Any address with cigargroup as part of it is linked to this group. Some of the Internet Cigar Group's more popular (and informative) sites include:

http://www.cigargroup.com/weblist/

This website lists cigar sites on the World Wide Web. When I last pulled it up, it included 249 sites, with information running the gamut from cigar-friendly and -unfriendly airports to personal pages posted by cigar lovers. Compiler Bob Curtis updates this site regularly. Asterisks highlight the more interesting noncommercial sites.

http://www.cigargroup.com/faq

A great source of general information, all about cigars.

http://www.cigargroup.com/cigar800.htm

A site listing the 800 numbers for contacting retailers, manufacturers, and distributors.

http://www.cigargroup.com/faq/health.htm

This site, compiled and copyrighted by Marc J. Schneiderman, M.D., summarizes the health information concerning cigars and smoking from a number of papers that have been published on these topics. Schneiderman's conclusion (which we cigar-lovers like) is that moderate/noninhaled cigar use poses no significant health threat.

http://www.cigargroup.com/where.htm

Planning a trip outside the United States? Check this site for information and locations of cigar shops worldwide.

Other Interesting Web Sites

http://www.fujipub.com/doublecorona.html

The Double Corona, a magazine on cigars published in Florida by Robert Langsam, maintains an on-line presence at this address.

http://www.netins.net/showcase/fujicig

This is the address for Fuji Publishing Group's Cigar Page, which is chock-full of information, links, and retailers. If you just go directly to this page and follow its links, you can save yourself a lot of time. It's an award-winning site and probably the best starting point for cigar information on the Internet.

http://www.cigarworld.com:80/

General Cigar Company maintains a great home page at this address, with lots of good information and links to other sites.

http://homearts.com/pm/shoptalk/12humif1.htm

Anyone thinking about building his or her own humidor should check out this site, which includes professional humidor plans from *Popular Mechanics*, the folks who know how to build everything (and will find out how to do it if they don't know). If you can't trust them, who can you trust?

9

Cigar Glossary

Barrel:	Another word for the body of a cigar.
Binder:	The leaf that holds the cigar together. It is rolled around the filler, under the wrapper.
Bloom:	A white, crystalline powder that sometimes forms on the surface of wrappers of cigars as they age. Not to be confused with mold, which actually permeates the wrapper.
Box-pressed:	Describes cigars that are actually pressed in their boxes, giving them a somewhat squared-off shape.
Bunch:	The leaves used to make up the filler and binder. They are bunched together, hence the name.
Cabinet box:	A cigar box without stickers or labels.
Cap:	The small piece on the head of the cigar, which is trimmed prior to smoking.
Cheroot:	A rustic-looking cigar, often medium to long in length and with a narrow ring size. Their wrappers tend to be rough or veiny.
Curly head:	A method of finishing the head of a cigar by giving the tobacco there a quick twist.
Divan:	A private smoking room or club.
Dress box:	The opposite of a cabinet box, the dress box is amply decorated with labels and other trimmings that cover the wood.

Dutch cigars:	A nonhumidified cigar. You'll also see them referred to as dry cigars. They are usually quite small in size.
Figurado:	Cigars with a figured shape, such as culebras, torpedos, bellicosos, and pyramids.
Foot:	The opposite from the head of a cigar. This is the end you light.
Goma:	The colorless, flavorless gum used to seal the wrapper on a cigar.
Handmade:	A cigar manufactured entirely by hand.
Hand finished:	A mostly machine-made cigar that has some hand work in the finishing process.
Hecho a Mano:	Made by Hand.
Keep:	Private cigar locker.
Marrying:	The blending of traits and characteristics between cigars. Sometimes desirable, especially when aging a number of similar cigars. Not desirable between a broad assortment of cigars with varying traits. Also referred to as aging.
Mold:	Maintain cigars in a too humid environment, and this is what you'll get. Different from plume as it permeates the wrapper of the cigar, spotting the cigar wrapper.
Puro:	A cigar whose filler, binder, and wrapper all are made with tobaccos grown in the same country. The word puro also means cigar in Spanish.
Ring size:	Used to measure the diameter of a cigar. Divided into one sixty-fourths of an inch.
Stogies:	Inexpensive cigars originally developed as a cheap smoke for settlers heading west. They were thought to resemble the spokes on a Conestoga wagon wheel. Today, a somewhat derogatory term for a cheap cigar.
Straight cigar:	A cigar that remains the same size from head to foot.
Tuck:	Another term for the foot of a cigar.
Wrapper:	The outside of the cigar.

INDEX